BLACK

What You Escape to

SHEEP

May Enslave You

DOWN

By Leah Joy Shaw

Black Sheep Down
By Leah Joy Shaw
Published by Leah Joy Shaw
© 2020 Leah Joy Shaw

I have tried to recreate events, locales and conversations from my memories of them. In order to maintain their anonymity in some instances I have changed the names of individuals and places.

ISBN #978-0-578-63461-6

For every soul that's ever felt unloved, unwanted or unworthy.

May these pages take you by the

hand and assure you that you

are not alone, forgotten or

unqualified to be everything

that your all-knowing and

infinitely loving creator has

made you to be.

Quench My Thirst

(Confessions of a Stripper)

My broken heart cripples me, as I stumble upon a stage.
My blood feels cold as sweat drips excessively down the
back of my knees. My clammy palms graze a metal pole in
an attempt to stop the trembling in my limbs. My eyes hit
the floor and suddenly I have a fear of heights.

Hungry, greedy eyes quickly surround me to catch my
falling grace. My naked flesh is served for only moments of
fulfillment until one's thirst is provoked once again. His
pleasures are granted to him only to be immediately
snatched away. Leaving him longing and anxiously
prowling for more of what he cannot sustain.

He sits like a fool at a wishing well, as he tosses his money and integrity into an illusion of cool quenching water. He admires his own reflection in its clear and tranquilizing surface. He dreams sweetly as I coax his vanity and watch him slip slowly beneath the subtle waves.

I wait patiently for his emotional submission as I distract him with each slither and sultry sway. When he reaches for breath, I will push him under. But not without seeing every man that should have loved me, the thief that stole from me, the liar who misled me, and each unsightly scar that still tarnishes my heart.

I proudly applaud my devious skill to profit from this illusion I've created of fresh running water in this dry and empty desert. This luring well has become my goldmine.

As I whet the palate, and scoff at the fool who threw his

money at a dry and empty well.

Yet his blood still stains my hands and his venom has

pierced through my skin. He reaches for me, but not to hold

me. He only desires to drink from my well. But his reach is

surely in vain. For, my well is dry, unlike this enticing pool

that his longing eye beholds. For this place is simply a

mirage, created with lights, and diluted perceptions, a

deliberate combination of eye candy for the restless soul.

He chews me up like sugar cane, until I recognize myself

no more. My reality becomes as oblivious and

misconstrued as that of the foolish man at the wishing well.

I turn my head in submission, as the gluttonous man feeds

and delights on the product of my emptiness. He fills his

tummy and quenches his thirst on the illusion of something

that dissolves into nothing and only continues to thirst for

more.

Table of Contents

Introduction

The Yoke

The yoke that I had carelessly toyed with had finally dropped down over my head and fastened itself tightly around my neck. Something that I once was able to slip in and out of on my own terms now imprisoned me. The price of its temporary relief from pain and spiritual thirst would become a debilitating debt collected directly from my soul. Pressing its unforgiving weight across my crumbling shoulders, forcing me to bear the relentless burden of my mistakes.

If you're wondering what in the heck a yoke is anyway, you're not alone. I always pictured the yolk of an egg whenever I heard it mentioned in church. But a "yoke" is actually used as a reference many times in the Bible referring to the harnesses used on animals around their necks. Jesus used many kinds of analogies, metaphors, and stories called parables to relate his teachings to what was familiar to his followers' daily lives and culture. But the thing is, most of us know little about farming, and the idea of a yoke goes way over our heads. So, let me fill you in.

The yoke was a heavy wooden contraption that would be fitted around the neck of an ox, which is why this particular animal has also been referred to as the "beast of burden." Oxen were controlled by this device to achieve the very grueling work of turning the earth and soil for the crops. The plow the oxen pulled was so heavy and big that they were the only animal strong enough to perform this daunting task. Such a large and strong beast can be difficult to yoke, so its master would begin to introduce it to the seemingly harmless device while the animal was still young and impressionable. As the ox grew, the only thing it knew was the yoke. So, what it obeyed in one season of its life, it was controlled by in another.

Jesus's purpose for using a yoke as a reference was to paint a clearer picture for us of the real, oppressive burden of sin on our lives. Imagine being bound by a device that literally turned your body from one direction to another without your consent! A contraption that forced you to go places you otherwise would never want to go.

Now, imagine someone approaches you and says, "Hey, I can free you from this barbarous and miserable life that I see you're stuck in. Let me just take this heavy thing that's digging into your neck and shoulders and destroy it with my superpowers." I mean, who wouldn't want that!

Whether we realize it or not, we do become a slave to our sin. The problem is we get so deceived by what the devil says about us, and what people say about us, that we actually learn to accept these living conditions as if we have no other choice. We are sons and daughters of the living God! We have value and purpose. We are cherished and loved. We are royalty in the kingdom of God! And yet often, here we are, being pulled and pushed around, living a life of oppression and slavery.

It shall come to pass in that day, that his burden

shall be taken away from your shoulder, and

his yoke from your neck, and the yoke will

be destroyed because of the anointing oil.

(Isaiah 10:27 NKJV)

My Personal Yoke

"I am going to write a book about all of this one day," I said as I lay in a man's bed sipping on a cocktail just after regaining consciousness from the several strong drinks I had consumed throughout the day.

"Do not use my name," he barked at me in his Arabic accent. My gaze then shifted lazily from an empty wall to a complete stranger standing over me, topping off my alcoholic beverage. I glanced around a room I was sure

I hadn't seen until that very moment when I asked the angry-faced man, "What is your name anyway?"

If it's not clear to you the state of mind I was in during the occasion described in the paragraph above, let me make it plain to you now: I was gone! I was absent from reality and had quietly excused myself from accountability. I was everything the magical world of intoxication would allow me to be. I was everyone and I was everywhere. I was home and I was safe. I was held and I was loved in the arms of anyone and everyone all at the same time. I was suspended in time. I was not early nor was I late. I was not too young nor too old. I was missing and briefly found and captured up into the wings of tranquility. It was a tranquility that covered me, and I held it close knowing all the while that its level of potency came at a painful price.

Soon the winds would begin to squeal a wicked horror through the trees while the dark clouds gathered and grew, swiftly chasing away the sweet embrace I'd known. My chemically constructed shelter would be ripped apart as the alcohol levels dropped in my bloodstream and evaporated from my pores. The withdrawal would swallow me up like a violent storm overtaking my body, my shoulders quivering and collecting the drops of rain spitting ruthlessly through the violent gusts of wind.

My stomach leaped at every crack of thunder in the sky, and I knew the end of my chemical escape was once again upon me. With great force it would grab me by the back of the neck, and the muscles throughout my body would painfully clench up in defense. The world around me seemed to pace excessively on my every nerve ending. Any glance that hit me was threatening and defeating to me. My blood felt as though it were curdling inside my veins as if tiny mites were crawling and biting just beneath the surface of my clammy skin. The phantom lovers that drifted in and out of my bed and imagination haunted my sanity.

Immediately, I began to run for relief from the furious storm swiftly chasing me.

I caught my vomit in my sleeve each time the stench of stale cigarettes and liquor were unleashed from the luggage that I unzipped. My secret stripper life was on wheels, toted and stashed with wrinkled lingerie shoved between pockets of empty cigarette packs and folded dollar bills. I would frantically rummage through a bag that shined a penetrating spotlight on a world that looked significantly better in the darkness of my denial. Just as sobriety would try to give me a closer look, I would quickly take some money and a few deep breaths in an attempt to attain the antidote for its rebuke. I slithered through a liquor store baring enough skin to distract the man behind the counter from my desperate demeanor (or so I thought). My sexuality was my mask and my lifeline. I used it when I needed it. But I needed alcohol to use it.

My plan of action in the event of the inevitable

storm of alcohol withdrawal was either complete seclusion

or sedation until intoxicated once again. To sedate the

storm was to calm the screaming and sirens that blared

violently in my head. My hands trembled so hard that I

could barely hold the bottle to my lips. Complete dread

consumed my body as I grudgingly forced each gulp of

straight-up liquor down my throat. My gut instinctively

refused the poison, yet I kept forcing it down until my gag

reflexes stopped. Until it was quiet again in my head. Until

I could breathe again. Until the terror and doom subtly

tiptoed to the back of my mind where I was only faintly

aware of its dreadful existence.

If I wanted to detox from alcohol completely, then I

would have to plan for absolute seclusion. This method

meant locking down the house and bracing for the storm. It

was as if I could hear the sirens blaring through the air

urging me to take cover. The idea of my symptoms

catching up with me in front of anyone was not only humiliating, but it would also reveal to everyone what I wasn't willing to admit yet. It would expose my fears, shame, and inability to prove I didn't need anyone else. It would inevitably unveil the heavy yoke that was now pulling me and driving me into such lunacy. As long as no one knew about my sickness, then it wasn't real and they wouldn't try to take something away that I didn't know how to give up. Instead, I sentenced myself to twenty-four hours of complete isolation in a dark room to be subdued by the consequences of my belligerent actions.

I crawled under my heaviest blankets as if they could hide me from the nasty monsters that would soon have their way with me. I braced my pillow for the vigorous shaking of my limbs and the grotesque illusions and graphic nightmares that had left me uncertain of my own reality. Shame snickered and snarled at me through each toss and turn. My ears still pounced from the bass that pumped through the club the night before. Much like the pulsating sounds that precede the imminent danger in a horror film, vague intoxicated memories shot like bullets through my skull, disgusting me and beating me brutally with each angry stone of shame.

Each time I closed my eyes, I didn't know where I was, or who I was with, until suddenly I would hear him yelling directly into the bowels of my ear canal. "LEAH!!!" he screamed at the top of his lungs. It was my father shouting my name with such urgency and authority in his voice, it startled me every time. It broke through my unconscious state and demanded me to wake up! I would shoot up in my bed, my eyes wide with the shock of how real he sounded though he wasn't even there.

This happened on countless occasions. I looked around the room where everything had suddenly just stopped—the pouncing in my ears, the graphic demonic dreams, and the daunting hallucinations. I would then curl up into the silence of the room and the heavy blankets now soaked in sweat, and pray repeatedly, "Dear God, I hate this. Help me please!" I cried like a prisoner caged in her own body, holding the keys but lacking the strength to use them to set herself free. I knew that I wanted to be set free from the yoke that was enslaving me, but I needed to be delivered from myself. From my desperation, my hurt, my shame, my weaknesses, but mostly from my unrelenting thirst for love and acceptance. A spiritual thirst that I eventually learned only God can quench.

In my best efforts to pray and ask for God's forgiveness, I was still convinced he was too repulsed and disappointed with me to love me ever again. I assumed that even if I stopped all of this reckless behavior, my mind would only ever be able to identify with the stripper that I had become. A role I planned to play just long enough to attain or get back what I felt was rightfully mine: the attention, affirmation, money, power, and freedom from dependency on anyone wanting to control me. Yet something *was* controlling me, as I couldn't seem to play this role long enough to attain all the things I felt I needed to take with me before I could move on with my life. I had been stolen from, lied to, cheated on, and spiritually shunned. Even God, who supposedly loves everyone, was certainly done with me. I had no idea what had become of me.

Hope was a mere sliver of light that slipped through the cracks of each door slammed in my face. I had a debt I was determined to resolve, and I was losing my ability to relinquish it from anywhere or anyone. Each payment made toward this delinquency was spent fast on the constant bandaging of my broken heart. All of the things that could only for a moment convince me I had power, control, and happiness through material things, men, and the boldness I found in alcohol.

I had convinced myself that I had no other choice than to sell my sexuality to survive financially, while in truth I used this environment to feel any value at all. I hated that I was so addicted to a lifestyle I *knew* was killing me, yet I couldn't imagine my life without it anymore. My enemy was now *me* and my own toxic desires. I began to assume that this twisted person who was quickly evolving inside of me must just be the real me, maybe all I had ever been and all that I could ever be!

But this was the lie the devil was counting on me believing. For as long as this was my truth, my life was spent in his dry, grueling field of hopelessness and shame. My head to the plow, face to the ground, crawling through the dirt and scum of life. My every move dependent on the one who had yoked me with the burden that was now driving me. His accusing words repeatedly assuring me that I was absolutely unacceptable of the love of my heavenly Father. The One who *destroys* the Yoke and *takes away* the burden also *quenches* the insatiable thirst of every longing

soul.

Chapter One

The Tares

There is a consistent voice speaking continually in the back of our minds. It's created from a combination of past experiences and words spoken to us or about us, causing us to assume we are being interpreted in certain ways in present life situations. It then becomes a story we tell ourselves about ourselves, which inevitably shapes our idea of who we are and what amount of greatness or failure we are capable of. I would compare this voice, or personal back story, to a weed that grows simultaneously and unintentionally with a flower or plant that one has planted in the ground. Someone may fertilize it and water it and yet be completely oblivious to the weeds that sprout up among its flowering blooms and fresh green stems. This comparison is much like the story in the Bible about a man who sowed good seed in his field, but while everyone was asleep, his enemy came and sowed tares, or weeds, among the wheat (Matthew 13:24–26).

While the people in my life who helped to cultivate me into who I was meant to be did in fact sow goodness, love, and godly principles into who I am today, the enemy—*our* enemy, the devil—sowed weeds among the good seed as he purposely planned to destroy me. Whether through the brokenness of those that had the most influence on me or simply through the default of living in a fallen world. In this book I am highlighting the power that these tares can have on our lives if not addressed and pulled out from our developing identities. Their consistent presence slowly creates unwanted patterns and disorienting emotions that we eventually identify with as our truth. This invasion of such a pestilent force can be found choking out the good character and beautiful destiny God has designed for our lives while sometimes appearing to look like the very thing it was assigned to disable. The tares in my life included shame, fear, inadequacy, and rejection, and they all led me into complicated relationships with my family and friends but mostly with myself and my perspective on who God is.

Weeds

My two older sisters stormed about the house with an exaggerated air of supremacy as my parents shut the door behind them to go on their yearly vacation to Florida. It was typical for them to team up against me when it was just the three of us. Regardless of who they were as individuals, they became their own kind of version of "Mean Girls" when they were together.

"What did you do with the money Mom and Dad left us, Leah?" my oldest sister asked with an accusatory tone as she rummaged through the glass cabinet where my parents had apparently hid the cash.

"I have no idea what you're talking about!" I barked back, feeling the two of them beginning to join forces against me.

"You took it! We know you did because it's not here!" My oldest sister's voice grew more agitated as she continued to shuffle around porcelain cups and decorative plates searching for the missing cash.

"I swear to you, I didn't even see it!" I continued to defend myself as they began to banter back and forth about what a liar I was and all the other reasons why I sucked at that particular moment.

"Well, that was the money they left us for food and gas, and now we're screwed," my oldest sister yelled as she slammed the cabinet door. Then they both marched off together complete with a hair swing and an eye roll.

To this day I have no idea who took the money. And to be honest, it didn't really matter. Although sometimes my middle sister would chum with me, I quickly realized that neither one of them were going to have my back that afternoon. This week would be about surviving the gloomy weather, the isolation I felt being stuck in the house, and my two older sisters being flat-out brats.

"Brett wants to come over," I overheard my oldest sister announce. "But I really don't want to hang out with him."

"Yeah, me either," my middle sister replied. "But it's whatever." She shrugged and continued, "If he comes over, we can just ditch him."

Now, Brett was that dorky guy from our church who always seemed to be around. Whether he was stopping by our house or hanging out at the church, he became like family in a sense. He was quite a few years older than my sisters and at least ten years older than I, so I viewed him more like a big brother than anything else. He was a tad flirtatious, but we always brushed it off as harmless charm. He would typically take my sisters out to dinner, and although I'm sure he sensed he was being used for a free meal, he never seemed to mind.

Sure enough, when Brett came over, my sisters took off and it was just him and me. His excessive compliments on my legs and backside were annoying, but I figured if I didn't react to them, he would eventually stop. I could tell he was annoyed by my sisters' quick bolt out the door, yet he stayed anyway. Of course, I was stuck there since at fifteen years old I didn't have a car or driver's license.

We sat and talked about the tattoos I wanted to get, the cigarettes I smoked that my parents didn't know about, and the non-Christian music I had hidden up in my bedroom. We conversed about boys and how just the thought of one putting his clammy hands on me completely grossed me out. It seemed every time I tried to be affectionate with a guy, there was just something awkward and nauseating about it. I just assumed I wasn't ready for it yet or I hadn't really liked anyone enough to enjoy it.

"You really need to get over that," he said. "That's not right."

"No I don't!" I laughed. "I'm perfectly fine with it."

"Seriously!" he persisted. "You need to be touched."

"Hey, do you want to take me out to eat?" I asked, trying to change the subject.

"Maybe, I'm not sure," he responded, as if he needed persuading.

"What are you not sure about?" I asked, confused by his hesitation.

"You need to get over this whole not being touched thing first," he said as he began to grab at my legs. I playfully pushed him away, trying to stay calm and cool, to prove to him and myself that I could handle myself in this kind of situation without making it uncomfortable or a big deal. Besides, if my sisters could handle his lewdness, why couldn't I?

Once I finally convinced him to leave to go eat dinner, I grabbed my jacket and jumped into his truck feeling just as important and mature as my older sisters. He climbed into the driver's seat next to me and immediately started grabbing at my legs again.

"C'mon," I pleaded. "Let's go! I'm so hungry!"

We finally made it to the restaurant, and as we pulled into a parking space, I quickly grabbed my door handle in an attempt to escape the vehicle before he started in on this touching thing again. "We just need to get inside with all those other people," I thought to myself, "and this whole weird touching thing will stop." But as I reached for the handle, he locked the door and said, "You're not getting out of here until you are touched." My stomach sank as his stubby fingers reached inside the giant holes of my '90s grunge-style jeans.

"Dude! C'mon, I really want to go in now," I pleaded once again, pushing his hands off my legs. "I said I was fine!" But my resistance seemed only to arouse him more as he began preying on the discomfort I felt and my fear of letting him know it. I wanted to be cool and capable of shooting down his advances without him seeing the anxiety jolting through my veins. But it was too late. He saw my fear, and he pounced on my discomfort like a tiger on its prey. Things went from awkward to disturbing as I felt a heavy weight of doom settle into my bones.

I stared up at a Red Lobster sign in defeat and embarrassment as my body lay still and subdued across the passenger seat of his red Dodge Ram. While his dreaded hands and fingers ventured where they wished, I could only disconnect from each one of my body parts as if they didn't matter to me anyway, in an attempt to just get through the daunting moment.

"Okay, I've been touched! Can we go in now?" I asked, not hiding my annoyance.

He reluctantly removed his busy hands from my body, unlocked the door and said, "We're not done helping you get over this, though."

My parents were gone for about a week, and Brett came over just about every day. Each day he was lewder and more persistent than the last. The final night was by far the worst, though. He rented a movie with several provocative scenes in it, and as the couple on the screen had sex, he asked, "Why don't you come over here?" He was lying on the couch, and I was purposely sitting on a chair across the room from him. I could tell he was aroused as he kept fondling himself periodically throughout the movie.

"I'm fine over here," I assured him, but he would *not* let up. If I didn't let him touch me, he would hold me down and tickle me until I wasn't sure which was worse— being violated sexually or tickle tortured. Finally, he pulled me on top of him and arranged my legs in a straddling position. He then proceeded to grab my hips and move me around on top of him while he watched the movie.

All the while, the sun was beginning to set outside as a sliver of fading daylight slipped through the windows into our house surrounded by empty fields. My mind began to race around the darkening living room walls, which seemed to close in on every attempt I made to avoid what was happening. Eventually I managed to pry myself off him exclaiming my sudden urgency to go to the bathroom.

As the night went on, so did the endless touching or tickling punishments. I remember thinking, "No one is ever going to come home!" as my eyes eagerly watched the time pass on a clock that sat on our wooden mantle just above the stone-embellished fireplace.

Finally, I became so riddled with anxiety and fear, it just burst out of every blood cell in my face. "STOP IT! GO HOME! NOW!" I screamed at him.

He gave me a long look as if to say, "What's your deal?" Like, what was wrong with *me*? Annoyed, he grabbed his things and left. But that wouldn't be the last time I would have to yield to the unwanted "touching" of this family friend. For the next few years, he would continue to prey on me in every dark corner of the church or quiet day at the restaurant I later worked at, sometimes alone. I was groped and felt up as if it were his right to touch me whenever he wanted to and in whatever way he wanted.

Unfortunately, the thought of telling anyone about Brett's behavior only seemed to pose a threat to myself and my collection of Tori Amos albums. He simply had too much dirt on me now! He knew about my cigarette smoking and the Jane's Addiction CD hidden in that Petra case on my bedroom bookshelf.

It wasn't until I had a boyfriend at seventeen that I realized something was really wrong with what Brett was doing. My boyfriend obviously became very mad when I confided in him about it. But to me Brett's inappropriate behavior had simply become, well, normal.

I didn't end up telling my parents about Brett until he became a suspect in my father's shooting, which happened just a couple days after my seventeenth birthday. Obviously, the police were looking under every rock to find the perpetrator, which of course included close friends of the family. At that point I thought I needed to share this side of Brett that they hadn't known.

I nervously confessed to my parents and older brother what had been happening with Brett. I felt my face fill up with heat and several shades of red as I explained the awkward details through giggles and fidgeting fingers. My brother, frustrated, said, "Why are you laughing? This isn't funny." He seemed confused and annoyed.

I was giggling because it was weird! It felt weird to hear my voice pull these words out of the hidden shadows and into the stark-naked atmosphere. Saying it out loud made it officially real when the weight of my confession consumed the expressions on my parents' faces. I was embarrassed, and somehow, I felt responsible for it since I'd never found the courage to stand up to it.

It was similar to the embarrassment I experienced with our family doctor who saw me through my teen years. He claimed he *had* to give me a breast exam whether I had the flu or a sprained ankle! (These were not your routine breast exams, by the way.) One day I went into his office to be tested for mono and of course received my usual very unique breast exam. As I was walking out of the room, I felt his hand reach deep into my pocket as he leaned down and whispered into my ear, "This is for you." Confused, I just nodded my head and proceeded to the lobby to check out with the oblivious girl behind the glass window. I walked out of the building as if I held a secret in my pocket. When I climbed into my car, I reached inside my pants to pull out a handful of Vicodin. A gift, I guess, for letting him inappropriately fondle my breasts as I lay there paralyzed by timidity.

I was angry with myself for being too spineless to confront my predators. All I could do in the moment was act as if nothing out of the norm was happening in hopes it would just be over soon. I was so embarrassed by my own fear and discomfort with them that I sacrificed my own dignity in an attempt to avoid transparency or confrontation. For some reason, I felt I had an obligation to appease or even protect my perpetrators from my objection to their abusive behavior. But it was clear they knew this, and it was exactly what they were feeding on—my submission to the wild, unforgiving, unrelenting tares of fear.

Chapter Two

Fight or Flight

Cameras flashed in our eyes as the smiles began to ache on our faces. I stood next to my oldest sister, Jennifer, in her long white wedding gown as we lined up for pictures following the wedding ceremony. The guests lingered about the large, decorated room, chatting and laughing with one another as guests typically do at a wedding reception. My proud parents were teary-eyed with joy as they watched my big sister begin her new life with her new husband. After an entire year of planning and prepping for "The Big Day" that had finally arrived, everything was absolutely perfect.

When I got home that night, my parents were sitting on their bed chatting about the highlights of the evening. My sister, Jodi, and I hugged them goodnight, then made our way into the bedroom next door to theirs. We eventually climbed into our beds, turned out the light, and fell asleep.

Suddenly something was pulling me out of my unconsciousness. It was a large noise followed by what sounded like a stampede of bulls charging down the stairs. My sister and I, half asleep in our beds, attempted to figure out the strange sounds, until I flipped back over and tried to fall back to sleep. But the noises wouldn't let me. I heard my father crying out in intense pain! When I finally opened my eyes, my mom yelled something my ears simply could not comprehend.

"Someone came in here and shot Daddy!" she announced in a strange, high-pitched voice, as she paced the floor between our bedroom door and her own.

"What?!" I crawled out of bed, only half coherently, and glanced into their bedroom. What I saw was something most people assume they will only view on film, maybe in a cop movie, but definitely not in their own home! Was I even awake? Was this simply a bad dream? But I couldn't seem to reopen my eyes in relief to find the comfort of reality. This *was* reality!

My body began to shake so hard I could barely stand. I sat down at the top of the stairs across from their bedroom feeling helplessly in shock. My mom then calmly asked my dad, "Do you know who did this to you?"

My father, struggling for breath, answered, "I don't know, I don't know."

"Call 911! Call 911!" my mom shrieked repeatedly.

My sister and I each picked up one of the house phones, but they were disconnected. My sister thought fast: since the church was right down the driveway from our house, she yelled from the bottom of the stairs, "Grab the church keys!"

My dad typically kept the church keys on his dresser, so as my mom entered their room and came out again, we assumed she had grabbed the church keys.

Instead, she climbed up and down the stairs several times with only the car keys in hand. We begged her to concentrate. When she finally handed my sister the keys to the church, my sister quickly left for help.

Immediately my mother turned to me and ordered me to stay with my wounded dad, groaning and dying before my helpless, frightened eyes. I hurried back down the stairs, trying to avoid the painful sight and confused as to why she wanted *me* to stay with him. I mean, she was a nurse, not to mention his wife! If anyone could save his life, it was her, right? "What can I do?" I thought. "I have no idea how to tend to bullet wounds, and I'm certainly not spiritual enough for God to answer *my* prayers!" But before I could make my case, she ordered me right back up the stairs and handed me a small towel for the bleeding.

I hurried back up to my dad and attempted to hold the cloth indecisively over each of the holes punctured in his pale flesh. He began to roll around on the bed, causing blood and fluid to spill out of him even faster!

"Please stop it!" I pleaded as he moved relentlessly, desperate for relief.

"I can't help it!" he cried in defeat.

I was officially useless in any practical way. All that I had was my faith in God and his ability to intervene in this desperate moment. I began to chant, "Jesus, Jesus, Jesus, Jesus," as many times as my dry tongue would allow me to speak over my dad's failing body.

"GOD, HELP ME!" he cried out several times, with the most anguished sound I had ever heard escape my father's vocal cords.

I stared out the large window as my eyes pleaded for the heroic arrival of lights and sirens racing down our long and winding driveway. But the view was just as hollow and bleak as the despair settling into my dad's voice.

His desperate cry for life began to fade into a darker plea. "I'm dying! I'm dying!" As I watched him, I believed that he was, and yet I was unwilling to accept my seventeen-year-old life without him in it. I refused to accept that God had simply abandoned us in that horrific moment without so much as a sense of his presence in this tragic injustice.

"But I need you! You can't leave me now!" were the only words I could find in my own attempt to postpone his dreaded good-bye. "God is here, Daddy!" my shaky voice pronounced, as if I was demanding Christ himself to find us and meet us in our misery and desperation. "He's here with you right now!" I shouted. But once these words passed from my lips, gasps for breath passed from his as he softly muttered his dying request.

"Serve Jesus," he repeated several times. "I love you, and serve Jesus."

My heart sank into a new realm of despair as hope seemed to slip with the color in his face and the fight in his voice, so I reassured him of my promise to follow through with his dying wish. "I know, Daddy, I know."

The absence of lights or sirens beaming through the bedroom window not only meant my father was not going to make it, but that my sister Jodi had been afflicted by the killer as well in her attempt to find aid. It was then that my mother came into the room with us and ordered me to run to one of the houses behind our property, to use their phone to call 911.

The next thing I knew, I was standing in the darkness outside, where a thick fog seemed to adorn the already chilling scene. My pajamas felt cold and wet as I stepped over the muddy ground beneath me. Terror consumed me as my trembling limbs battled with the urgent command to run through a dark open field where a malicious killer had just tread on his way to murder my father. My eyes fiercely probed the land in each direction, anticipating bullets perforating my body at any moment. My eyes caught a small porch light looming from a home in the distance, and suddenly I was running. I ran as if bullets were chasing my frantic little legs. I sprinted through tall, sharp weeds and wet, sticky mud until my fists landed on the front door of our neighbor's house.

I pounded and cried out, but there was no response. Frantic, my eyes searched for more porch lights. When I arrived at the next house, I banged on the door as hard as I could, gasping for air, thick as it was around me. As the man opened the door, I immediately sobbed, "Someone shot my dad! You need to call 911 NOW!" The stranger stood there for a moment confused, then with an expression of disbelief picked up the phone and began to dial 911. I quickly glanced around my neighbor's house, then made a beeline for the kitchen. I raced through his cupboards, turned on the faucet, and helped myself to a glass of water without the stranger's permission. My mouth was unbelievably dry. The man then informed me that the call had already been made about our emergency and offered to drive me back to my house. As we pulled into the driveway, I noticed the police and fire department had finally arrived, and my hand quickly reached for the handle to exit the still-moving vehicle.

When I ran up to the house, I realized my sister had also returned, but the cops had to scope out the house before anyone else could come inside. Soon EMS went racing up the stairs as my mom, my sister, and I stood anxiously in the middle of the living room floor.

As they carried my father down the stairs on a stretcher, my sister shrieked, "I love you, Daddy!" She jumped up and down uncontrollably as my mother and I just stood there in tears. He removed his oxygen mask and responded with a whisper, "I love you too." With that the paramedics carried his body out the front door, into the ambulance, then eventually out of sight. The screaming

sirens and bright lights flailed through the darkness and

into the unknown new trajectory of our lives.

My mind was searching for consolation as my

stomach began to ache and turn with anxiety and despair. I

tried to picture what my dad's crown would look like in

heaven. "Would it have extra jewels on it?" I thought to

myself, considering he was a pastor and all. "What would

eternity look like for my dad?" I honestly did not think he

would survive.

Soon the dark night faded into a dawn that painted

the sky in a dull and dreary shade of gray. My sister Jodi

and I clasped hands and stepped into what seemed like

another world. My eyes caught a clutter of emotion that

quickly surrounded us and squeezed us hard. We continued

through a tunnel of hugs and "I love you's" from family

and friends had already arrived at the hospital. My face felt

numb and my eyes were heavy in their sockets. Just being

in a hospital felt reassuring, though the odds of survival were still very slim.

When the surgery was finally over and I could see my dad, I just assumed he was fixed. You know, like in the movies when someone gets shot, they go to the hospital, have surgery, then wake up and casually converse with their visitors.

I raced into his room and my heart immediately stopped.

"What's wrong with him, Mom?" I asked. She was calm as she tried to explain the medication he was on to keep him stable, but all I could focus on was his pale swollen body shaking and jolting vigorously on the hospital bed. It appeared that at any given moment the convulsing would stop and he would be gone. His body was attached to an endless variety of machines and tubes, all committed to keeping him alive.

That night my whole family decided to sleep in the waiting room at the hospital. I, on the other hand, wanted to run as far away from my grief as I possibly could. I spent that night at a friend of the family's house, thinking that having space away from the cause of the pain might alleviate it somehow. When I woke up the next morning, the sun was bright, almost cheerful, and the air was cold and crisp. It was as if yesterday's tragedy had been contained to the gloom that it was physically encased in. The aroma of fall filled our friends' cozy neighborhood as I opened the front door and planted myself on the front porch. I absolutely loved fall and I loved sitting outside to daydream in its tranquility. This morning, however, I planned just to sit and take in everything that had happened the day before. I wanted to find my own emotional bearing, and this seemed like the perfect spot to do so.

As I glanced around at the matching houses and the cars that periodically drove by, a strange sense of suspicion began to creep into my thoughts. I remembered that I was supposed to be "hiding" until the gunman was found and taken into custody. "Could he be watching me?" I thought. "Would he really be able to find me, and would he shoot me right here on this cement porch?" Suddenly I felt like a deer during hunting season. I was sitting in clear view under this brightly lit, crisp autumn sky just waiting for a gun full of bullets to be unleashed on all my vital organs!

Finally, I couldn't take it anymore! I ran inside as my heart palpitated violently in my chest. I paced excessively around an empty house, but there was nowhere to go. Each window, every dark corner, the space behind each shower curtain brought on dread and the powerful persuasion of my imagination. It was as if a switch had been turned on in my psyche that caused each thought to assume, I was in some kind of danger. I could have never imagined how *this* would become a new normal for me. That I would spend the next several years oppressed by a sense of great doom that would have me second-guessing normal things like sitting in front of windows, walking down a nature path, or even sitting alone at a traffic light.

A New Normal

The days thereafter occurred in a time zone all their own. I felt I was stuck in a world completely torn and isolated from the rest of the "normal" world—or what seemed at the time, the oblivious world. My dad miraculously survived the ounce of lead that had ripped a three-inch hole into his chest from a twelve-gauge shotgun. My family and I were beyond grateful to God, as it was an absolute miracle that he survived at all! He spent several days in the ICU, and when he was eventually released from the hospital, our family went into hiding. We stayed in the guest home of someone who had been attending our church for years. Finally, we decided to go home, as we had no idea when the shooter would be caught and we obviously couldn't hide forever. But home took on a completely new norm, as we all seemed to be waiting for the shooter to return and accomplish what he attempted to do the morning he fled our property.

Although the police investigation was in full swing, it seemed they were pointing their fingers in all the wrong directions, including mine, and I found myself a potential suspect in my own father's shooting. It was the first and only time I had experienced any sort of interrogation, besides the probing of my parents, of course. The good cop, bad cop game is a *real deal* that left me feeling victimized not only by the shooter but by the aggressive accusations of the detectives as well. I guess my truth didn't prove to be true enough for them, for the next thing I knew I was being driven to a private facility to take a lie detector test. I couldn't understand why I was the only family member being singled out as a potential suspect. Did the cop's sense that I was the black sheep of the family and somehow assume that would make me a psycho criminal?

During those months of the investigation, bedtime at my house looked like something out of a refugee documentary. Everyone slept in the living room except for me. I guess I longed for "normal" so much that I tried my best to create it by simply returning to my bedroom to sleep in my own bed at night. My mom would sleep on the couch, my dad in a recliner, my sister on the floor, and, of course, a volunteer guard with a shotgun in a chair. Security alarms were set, doors were triple locked, and items that could possibly be used as defense weapons were strewn across the floor or kept in the tight clutches of a family member.

This would be our new normal for almost a year as we waited on our freedom once the shooter would be detained. The only thing we could aspire to detain ourselves was our fear. The shooter was never found, but our freedom would have to be. The journey through fear's dark, deep demise would prove to be conflicting and frustrating for all of us, to say the least. For me it became a sounding alarm whose volume, I would eventually discover, I could lower with alcohol. It would be an empty hole that I would try to fill with the affections and companionship of others. It waited grudgingly on every corner, and it was clingy and vulnerable in every relationship. I wouldn't completely confront *this* fear until I confronted all the other tares that had shot up and wrapped mercilessly around the person God had created me to be. Until then I would cohabitate with its lies, its torment, and the powerless feeling of being subjected to its ruthless authority over my life.

Chapter Three

Broken Girls Fall for Broken Boys

When I became aware of my desire for connection
and intimacy as a teenage girl, I stood puzzled at the
inevitable crossroads of my well-ingrained belief system.
When my curiosity of the subject of sex surfaced in my
parents' ears, they quickly pulled the blinds, locked the
doors, and rebuked every devil in our parsonage home!
Okay, not really. But they did seem to chastise and avoid
the uncomfortable conversations as opposed to just having
them.

As I grew older, I began feeling weighed down
under the shadow of a steeple that seemed to govern and
dictate more and more. I would start to wonder why I never
seemed to fit the clichéd mold of Christianity as my holy
crayons always slipped outside the lines and my interest
wandered outside of its box. While frowned upon for their

carnality, my likes and dislikes seemed just as relevant and real to me as the heartbeat inside my chest.

I felt that I disappointed my father for my lack of conformity or charismatic behavior in church. I couldn't fake God out or anyone else. I had watched so many people put on their Holy Ghost show to achieve a status symbol in the church or brownie points with the leadership that it just became a huge turnoff to me. While I took great pride in my father's title and the nobility that it stood for, I felt it also required something of me that my confidence couldn't seem to deliver.

Although my love and honor for God was embedded deeply inside my heart, my faith in him was simply through my parents. I assumed God's love for me wavered just as easily and often as my father's humanity surfaced in our parsonage home. Unable to sustain any lasting approval from my family or church, I just assumed there must be something wrong with me as I began to explore perspectives outside the confines of my parent's say-so. When the opportunities presented themselves, I would run into the world's mischief like a little kid through the streets of Disneyland! The wilder and crazier of a ride I could get myself on, the more confident and liberated I felt.

When it came to sex, the only concept I understood about it was explained to me by my teenage boyfriends. Their interpretation of sexuality was not only all I knew but became what I eventually needed to feel value, power, or any validation at all.

I found myself clinging to boyfriends to define who I was, embedding my soul in the safe haven (aka codependency) of these relationships. When they ended, I was destroyed. All I could see of myself were random pieces of a story dispersed into a whirlwind—unlikely, I assumed, ever to settle and collect into one whole person after the shredding of a union that had bound together my own existence. Even if the relationship was toxic or even dangerous, I held on with fierce loyalty, desperately believing my lover's faithfulness would return to me. I blamed myself for being fooled, for being naïve, but mostly for being so thirsty for love and even spiritual communion with another.

Before my first love, Nick, I struggled to stay interested in a boy for much longer than a week. So, when I became immediately infatuated with him, naturally my sixteen-year-old mind assumed that he must be "the one"!

Now, Nick had a whole lot of issues of his own to manage. He suffered from a bipolar disorder, and the violent pink scars that ravaged the pale undersides of his wrists and forearms told tales of his emotional torment. His scars cried out for help, attention, and awareness of his suicidal thoughts. He was sweet. He was cruel. And of course, just a teenage boy. We had been dating for just a couple months before my dad was almost murdered, so the aftermath of my crisis immediately placed him in a position in my life that far exceeded his emotional capacity. He was the last person I had spoken with that night and also the first person I called when it happened. I clung to this manic-depressive roller coaster for dear life; while he was wavering on his own flimsy branches of sanity, I looked to him as a means of keeping mine.

I deeply loathed the aftermath of the crime committed to my family, as it seemed almost as dark and isolating as the event itself. My family and I replayed the details over and over again on a daily basis. We had adjusted our lifestyles and perspectives to an unknown agenda of an unknown and uncaught killer. I felt caged in the desolate atmosphere due to the new heightened security measures in our lives. My independence had been extremely restricted before this event, but afterward it seemed like I would be on complete lockdown until the gunman could be taken into custody.

The only person I was allowed to hang out with

during this time was my boyfriend, Nick, and even then I could only leave the house for short periods of time. He became my escape, whether he was pulling up in my driveway or just existing in brighter thoughts, as I fought so hard to forget the gloominess around me. This oblivious boy took my hand and fed a blind girl's dreams with beautiful words and empty promises. He was completely clueless to the life-or-death sustenance he was serving his hungry audience.

Nick's role in my life was not just that of a teenage boyfriend but a knight in shining armor who I hoped could pick me up and whisk my shame and insecurities away into happily never happened. As if I could foot him the bill of each unpleasant transaction placed on my account, in exchange for my innocence and undying loyalty. I was committed to who he was, whether good or bad, manic or depressive. I would sacrifice my soul to this young man in hopes his affirmation would be just enough to quench a thirst that was already beginning to taunt me.

Yet his beatings on the same frail places would just leave bigger holes. My immense desire for sanctity would only become stronger as I sought out more aggressive ways to treat such a powerful thirst.

When I turned nineteen years old, I moved into an apartment with Nick, and our fights only became more devastating and belligerent. One night after a good, open-handed swing to my face, I went ahead and filed a police report. With the restraining order in place, I was forced to move on with my life and begin my withdrawal from my addiction to Nick. I was still nineteen years old, but this time I was on my own. I was living in my own apartment and had become a full-time student at a massage therapy school.

To keep my mind from wandering back to my freshly severed relationship, I relished in my newfound freedom from my overbearing parents and my unhinged boyfriend. I had given up on appeasing my family or experiencing a healthy "normal" relationship with a guy. I was convinced that if I removed all intimate emotions from sex, I could undermine its power to create a spiritual connection between me and the one I believed would desert me eventually anyway.

Whatever You Escape to Will Eventually Enslave You

I didn't fall in love with my second boyfriend, Rex, right away, as he swung in on the same wind of Nick's exit from my heart. Besides, I had chosen to indulge in a promiscuous lifestyle—the only lifestyle I deemed suitable for my polluted perspective on love—so now I figured I would turn the tables and take control over these emotions that were so inconveniently connected with sex.

Rex grew up on the very opposite side of the tracks from myself, so to speak, and his uninhibited upbringing intrigued me. His appetite for partying and his free ride to do so were definitely the initial ingredients to winning my heart. Since I was struggling to pay for my new independent life as a student and adult care giver, he said he knew a great way to compensate for my lack of means to make it on my own. He suggested I work as a shot girl in a strip club in Chicago where his friend was a bouncer. Rex exposed me to all the things I had only wondered about prior to our relationship. It was a much dirtier and colder world out there than the small, catty town I had called home. I was completely terrified, yet strangely fascinated, by these forbidden flavors of life that were now so abundant around me.

When we walked into the topless venue for the first time, I was immediately fascinated by the uninhibited atmosphere and yet strangely uncomfortable with the detachment in the girls' eyes and the hardness that hung wearily across the faces of those working there. The entire scene made me feel sad and mischievous all at the same time. There was a part of me that wanted to know the secret to severing the emotions that had previously left me feeling vulnerable and brokenhearted. These people seemed to have accessed the liberating power found in detaching sentiment from sexuality, and I was definitely intrigued. The other part of me saw all the lost sheep I grew up learning about in Sunday school. I remembered the colorful illustrations of Sodom and Gomorrah in my children's Bible. I remembered the defiance and self-indulgence that the detailed sketches conveyed, of a people living without reverence or restraint. As the pages from my children's Bible were trying to tell me one thing, my brokenness was saying another. So, I made a decision to do what I thought was compromising between the two: I would benefit from a job that I swore to God I would never give myself to completely.

Selling shots in a strip club proved to be extremely difficult on me *and* my liver. I never imagined that I would have to drink most of the shots I sold and end up puking my brains out just about every night I worked. Finally, one evening, while I was pedaling shots of pucker around the crowded club, I was asked to go onstage. My stomach fluttered nervously, but my eyes lit up with the thrill. Immediately I knew I would never pick up that sticky tray of shots again.

I found stripping to be exhilarating and exciting as my only job requirement was to be glammed out and ballsy enough to dance around half naked. Plus, I could smoke and drink as much as I wanted while doing it. I felt powerful as well as disconnected from love and other people's feelings. But I also felt strangely isolated and distrusting of everyone around me.

My brief stripping endeavor, however, came into conflict with my now six-month relationship with Rex. Since he had developed feelings for me, stripping was not an option for me, according to him. So, grudgingly I quit the topless gig and opted for a second chance at love instead.

This new love was full of so many qualities my previous relationship had lacked and yet would prove to be just as toxic as the last. Although the weeds around this new garden looked different, they were still weeds, popping up everywhere, and they continued to starve any healthy ideas of what a real, intimate relationship should look like.

What confused me about Rex was that he really did seem to care for me. He did everything my other boyfriend didn't. He bought me lunch every day, attended church with me and my family every Sunday, and seemed genuinely committed to me. To us. Yet there always seemed to be something wrong with me. It seemed we spent hours upon hours discussing all of my aggravating faults and physical flaws. He took care of me like a nurturing father yet also critiqued and shamed everything I did. Of course, he ended up cheating on me and becoming physically abusive, but I can't help believe that I stayed

with him to prove something to myself about myself.

Although I knew the way he was treating me was wrong, I

refused to fail at being his girlfriend! I couldn't end it with

him believing that I was as incompetent as he said I was.

Where would the justice be in that?

Getting Justice In Rejection

One night we went out to a party with a friend of his

who would eventually become my first husband. Rex was

off flirting with girls and ignoring me as usual, and I ended

up spending most of the night hanging out with his friend

Ryan. Ryan was this super easygoing, kind of awkward

guy. He was slightly overweight, maybe not a lady's man

but easily a friend of the ladies. His round face and bright

green eyes held a childlike innocence and demeanor that

immediately disarmed those who engaged with him. (Think

SpongeBob SquarePants.) Ryan became the third wheel on

quite a few occasions as the three of us hung out together, although he never seemed to mind.

Several months after my breakup with Rex, I ran into both of them at a local bar where I stopped in one night on my way home from a salon I was assisting in at the time. Of course, I ignored my ex-boyfriend and ended up talking to Ryan the entire night. We both joked and mischievously giggled about how jealous Rex seemed to be of us talking, and I believe we both relished in his irritation for our own reasons. I'm sure Ryan was sick of being the less desirable one out of the two of them, and I simply wanted Rex to see that I was still wanted. Just because he didn't find value in me anymore did not mean that I didn't have any. This would end up being the first night of mine and Ryan's story together as it took off with full force immediately afterward.

Ryan pursued me like a rare jewel, and I collected all of his validation and acceptance as any gluttonous lover would. He then paraded me around as if to make a statement to every other girl who never gave him a second look or to the friends who'd left him in the dust as *they* always seemed to get the girl. Although this relationship seemed convenient for both of us, I believe it was a bandage we both used to cover our own personal insecurities and brokenness as if it could be enough.

Chapter Four

Identity Down

All of us sat up straight in our seats as the principal of our Christian school came to visit our second-grade classroom one afternoon. Every child was on his or her best behavior when she very sweetly asked the students, "Now, do any of you children know what you would like to be when you grow up?" My arm swung up into the air as high as I could reach, my fingers sprang from my hand, and my eyes pleaded with her to call on me. When she finally did, I responded without hesitation.

"I am going to be a missionary when I grow up!" I blurted out proudly. She nodded and smiled with approval, then moved on to the next child waiting to answer.

I'm not even sure I knew how to multiply or divide at that point, but I *knew* that God had called me into ministry. When your father is a pastor, ministry is your life!

Maybe that's why I had come to this conclusion about my destiny at such a young age. Or maybe it had something to do with that time when I was about six years old and this sweet little old lady came up from behind me at the altar one Sunday evening and began to prophesy over me. She told me how God was going to use me to go into other countries and speak to people in other languages about Jesus.

Of course, by the time I got to middle school this whole idea of God calling me to do something significant for him began to seem more and more far-fetched. While I still had a deep respect for church and love for God, anything that had to do with either began to feel very forced and somewhat hypocritical. The thing about being a pastor's kid is, although you may have full access to all the goodies in the church pantry, you are also exposed to all of the church's dirt and unavoidable politics. The drama and humanity of it all can create a dreary film over the lens of one's expectations of Christianity as well as the people who call themselves Christians. I watched both church members and staff whom I once looked up to speak critically of my father's leadership and character and even try to divide the church we were all giving our lives to.

There is also a weight placed on a preacher's kid. I couldn't help but feel responsible for my father's ministry. If my worship as a teenager didn't resemble the ideal expression of worship to God in a church service, then how did that make the youth group look? Better yet, how did that make my dad look? How could I have an authentic Christian walk when my authenticity had to be second to my performance? At least the pressure made it seem that way anyway. If I could not perform, then I was ultimately failing everyone, including God. This had me questioning who I was and what I was really made for. I clearly did not fit into the cookie-cutter ministry ideal, so I wondered where I fit in as a Christian at all.

At eighteen years old, I decided to go to massage therapy school. Soon after I finished, I realized that as long as I wasn't a student anymore, I couldn't stay on my parents' health insurance plan. Well, I certainly was not making enough money with my massage therapy certificate to provide for my own health coverage. So, I took a sudden interest in going to cosmetology school. Besides, doing hair just seemed more "me" than grazing people's freckles and enlarged pores to the sounds of Enya and the smell of lavender and chamomile.

Although I had finally found something I loved to do, at twenty-one I was still shuffling through the discontentment of shallow relationships and superficial endeavors, aching for real purpose and significance in my life. As I continued to navigate through my early twenties, my insecurities and the pressure I felt to be a "good Christian" still weighed on me. I felt as though I failed God with every other breath I took or with the disappointment that hung on my parents' faces.

During that season I made a lot of frivolous choices in an attempt to find my purpose. I wanted something I could slap on my shirt and proudly wear like a name tag and just point to it whenever anyone inquired, "What are you doing with your life, Leah"? I felt like I had to hurry up and call my life something so that I could be remotely relevant to society. This is the very reason I married my first husband Ryan at twenty-four years old. I wanted to be taken seriously. I wanted something I could physically point to that would identify me. I wanted the never-ending questions to end in my head that screamed, "What is my purpose in life?!" As if getting married would stop them.

Purpose

When I jumped into marriage, I figured I might as well jump into motherhood as well. "This is it!" I thought.

This is what my purpose is! To be married, have babies and a house with a white picket fence. But to my surprise, pregnancy turned out to be an incredibly humbling and lonely time. I never realized how much of my identity and value were tied up in the way I looked, as my body completely transformed into something I never imagined, and so did the marriage I thought I could predict. I looked different, I felt different, and it seemed my husband treated me completely differently as well! He became very distant and cold, and with every pound I gained, I felt my value to him diminish in his disapproving eyes. Suddenly the one who was once bandaging old relationship wounds had become a present perpetrator of them.

His pursuit of my commitment had come to a screeching halt as the endless feeding trough of praise and validation was snatched abruptly from my thirsty lips. His adoration of me was painfully replaced with a deep disdain and an unsettling attempt to control. Desperate for spiritual nourishment, albeit through another person, I began to pursue him in our union by aspiring to have the perfect body, planning more date nights, and basically doing anything I could think of to get his affections back on me.

But my quest for Ryan's reassurance would only drive him further away. Suddenly all the little things that seemed to make our pretty picture complete began looking more like the constructs of a prison than my happily-ever-after. The house with the white picket fence was way out of our means, as we struggled to make the mortgage every single month. Our bills began to stack up against us as did our offenses and our ability to see past them.

Although we had similar convictions when it came to marriage and family, our core was still dependent on superficial demands rather than any godly, spiritual pursuit together. Our union lacked everything I felt in my gut it should have. It soon became evident to me that I had compromised what I knew a marriage should be for a quick resolution to my inadequacies, insecurities, and thirst for approval.

By the time I was about to give birth to our daughter, I was completely discouraged with the whole idea of marriage and every single major life decision I had made up until that point. When we drove to the hospital early that morning to have our baby, a beautiful rendition of "Somewhere Over the Rainbow" by Tori Amos played fittingly in the background of the otherwise silent drive to the delivery room. With my belly pushed up against the dashboard of my tiny car, I stared out the window as tears rolled silently down my cheeks. There I was with my husband, about to meet our little girl, and nothing looked or felt like I thought it was supposed to.

Almost ten hours later miss Lily Joy was born, and something inside me was born as well! Although I was a new mom still figuring everything out, I was completely obsessed with my little girl. I would just hold her and stare at her for hours and weep. I was surprised to discover that having a baby was this incredible spiritual experience for me. It was miraculous and beautiful. I couldn't take my eyes off my child because to me she represented God's existence and his handiwork manifested through *my* body. I felt so incredibly special, and although I was still discouraged about my marriage, I was also completely enthralled and preoccupied with my little princess.

I was a stay-at-home mom for almost two years with my daughter while Ryan was either working or traveling. Lily and I became extremely close as it was just the two of us most of the time. I recorded every small milestone and every sweet moment in between. I journaled about her, wrote poetry about her, and soaked up every moment of her little life as it definitely seemed to swallow up all of mine. I had found my purpose in loving and nurturing this child, and it created a bond between us that I had never imagined I could know.

To End A Marriage...

As my marriage proceeded to deteriorate, I began to seek out reasons and voices to validate the decision to file for divorce. Once that decision became final, my hurt and disappointment taunted me, and I began to seek out people and places that could distract me from the disorienting emotions that come with leaving a marriage.

About six months into our separation, it was near wintertime in Illinois and my heart felt as empty and abandoned as the dark sky that seemed to creep in all too early across every afternoon. I had spent the entire summer running from the emotions that came from severing my marital vows. I had been going out for drinks with the girls, getting wasted at parties, and hooking up with random guys who for a moment made me feel wanted and maybe even optimistic about finding new love. But as summer and then fall began to collapse into the brittle limbs of the November trees, so did all the festive distractions that postponed my inevitable grief. I was now forced to come face-to-face with my decision to end my marriage and take responsibility for all the bridges I had burned ensuring I couldn't go back to it even if I tried.

I didn't want to return to my husband necessarily, but the silence of solitude was deafening. I began to wonder if being in a miserable relationship was easier than being left alone to sort through the endless rubble from its bitter collapse. I felt isolated and forgotten as I spent the last few months of our separation alone in a house that felt more like a grave site at this point than a home. Our belongings had been torn in half by several obnoxious fights. (I'm sure the neighbors were entertained.) Half of the furniture was gone, as boxes and pictures were strewn across the floor like the aftermath of any catastrophe. Yet I continued to live amongst the wreckage, refusing to pick up any of its broken pieces, as the disarray only mirrored the condition of my soul.

I didn't know who or what I identified myself with anymore and exactly how to move forward. I underestimated the stigma attached to being a divorcée with a kid and just how that would change the way some people would perceive me. I wasn't prepared for the looks I would get with my ringless finger and a child in tow. I never imagined how being a single mom would severely decrease my value in the dating world as my past read more like a negative credit score than a person with anything left to offer someone else. Unfortunately, this only reiterated all of the insecurities I had been running from my whole life.

I went from thinking I had arrived in my purpose and self-worth only to settle for small doses of validation in different men's glances, flattering words, and bedroom invitations. It seemed I was wrong about so many things and I questioned what else I could be oblivious to. I didn't know whom to believe in anymore, and I certainly didn't believe in myself. I wondered how this divorce would change the dynamics of my relationship with my daughter, as all of the variables in our lives were on the verge of change. The only real purpose I had left in my life was my little girl and the honest faith she still had in me, which I could hardly find in myself.

Chapter Five

Striking the Stone

My divorce had only been finalized for a few months. I moved into my parents' partially finished basement with my daughter, as the house my husband and I lived in was lost in the financial destruction of our divorce. Everything I seemed to identify myself with was crumbling quickly into a disaster that I couldn't bear to look at, let alone recover from.

If a divorce wasn't confusing enough, moving back home with your parents who still treat you like a bothersome teenager certainly is. I was staying there with my mom, dad, sister, and her child. So when I arrived with my two-year-old daughter, my hope was that our family dynamics in this new situation would go as smoothly as it did for my sister living there. Unfortunately, this was absolutely not the case. I became the youngest and the black sheep of four children once again, and my child was just an extra sibling thrown into the mix. The relationship lines were completely blurred, and I waited anxiously for the moment my motherhood role could be restored to me and possibly my adulthood as well.

I began working two jobs: hair stylist by day and cocktail waitress by night. I was exhausted but determined to save up enough money to move out on my own with my daughter.

But the loneliness plagued me, and the family that had applauded me for pulling myself out of an abusive marriage now seemed disdainful of my presence and undermining of my parenting. I was aching inside, but instead of giving my family and my thirst for approval over to God, I was still completely unable to separate God from my family. With my worth still dependent on others, I was feeling desperate to run somewhere, anywhere to ease the pain of my broken heart. To be, if only for a moment, received and briefly quenched by someone or something. Even if it meant waking up the next morning to a stampede of Bible thumpers thundering down the basement stairs. Which is exactly what happened one particular Sunday morning.

"Does Anybody See Her"

My mother's high heels clicked with force, as someone was smacking their peppermint gum. I could smell the wave of cologne and hairspray hit me before their anger ever did. I was certain last night's cocktails still lingered on my breath, as did the cigarette smoke in my tangled hair. I had already been beating myself up for my stupid lapse of reasoning the night before. In fact, I had already reassured myself what a loser plus slut I was. I realized if I were a good person, I would have been primped, polished, and parading around in my church dress thirty minutes ago! But there wasn't enough makeup, perfume, or breath mints for me to hide behind this time.

My heart felt just as sick as the faint traces of dry martini still pooling together in my queasy stomach.

As I sat up in bed to face my retribution, the three of them closed in around me. Their furious tongues lunged at me as if they could will a punch or two with each crippling word. Their voices united together to ambush their prey into conformity, into conviction. They were trying to break down something that was already broken. They were only willing to accept who they thought *they* would be in my shoes—or who they thought I *should* have been in my shoes. Heck, I wasn't even sure how to put these new shoes on, let alone walk in them! I was just as frustrated and disappointed with me as anyone. I began to cry relentlessly. Not just because of their rebuke or the mistake I'd made sleeping with a man I hardly knew the night before. Instead, these tears were my white flag waving in surrender. "This pain is bigger than me! Help me! I am on the verge of falling completely apart here!"

"Mothers don't go on dates!" my father exclaimed, his angry face reaching toward mine as if to challenge me to respond. Cowardly, I sank as deeply into the seams of the mattress that the bed would allow. It was as if I was reaching for my heart as it fell into a whole new realm of despair. Not only had I lost myself in this divorce, but I had lost my God as well. I was certain he was with them, not me, after they told me what a disgrace I was, gathered their Bibles, and left for church.

When the front door shut behind them that morning, something in my heart closed on them as well. I was convinced I had nowhere to turn to anymore. It seemed life's only options were simply what kind of pain could I suck up and manage to survive. I immediately began scrambling through a list of broken relationships in my head, eagerly planning an escape from my present situation. The fierce adrenaline igniting all the other heightened emotions I was flailing in became the perfect cocktail for frivolous choices and desperation. It seemed every well I turned to drink from was either polluted or toxic in one way or another.

I had always been so dependent on the fierce loyalty and substance of a relationship. Without trust or sentiment toward another person, life seemed absolutely maddening to me! I racked my brain for yet another out. Another reaction to the previous reaction to the previous reaction. That was basically the endless cycle that was beginning to define my life. I didn't rest in God, nor did I trust him to work *anything* out for my good. I still thought God had something to do with those sharp, angry fingers in my face from just a few moments before.

My ex-husband at this point wasn't even contacting us anymore, let alone supplying any of our daughter's needs. He had moved in with a woman and her son seven hundred miles away soon after our separation.

Still, I was desperate for a voice to validate my hurt. I was looking for a savior and it was slim pickings.

When I decided to contact Ryan, he reassured me that I was a great mother and my family was just trying to take my child from me. He suggested I move down to Georgia where he could be a father to Lily. He promised to begin paying his court-ordered child support payments so that we could afford to live down there once I arrived. I told him I would never have enough money saved up in time to move. He suggested I just become a stripper for a few months and save up the money that way. I laughed and said, "Right!"

"You've done it before!" he pressed, as he was familiar with my very brief history of working in a strip club several years before we were married. "Seriously! You can do this!" he said. "It's for your child! I will come to pick her up in a few days and you can meet us down here in a few months."

Suddenly I was feeling strangely empowered, understood, and, well, not alone anymore.

When my family returned home from church, they were immediately apologetic toward me. They explained how they heard a song at church called "Does Anybody Hear Her," and it convicted them of their critical words with me just before the service. The song, written by a band called Casting Crowns, is about a girl desperately seeking love in all the wrong places. When she finally chooses to seek love and acceptance at a church, she is snubbed and judged by the people there. The main message in the song explains how our purpose as Christians is to reach out and love those who are broken and hurting. Not to judge or shame them.

When they were finished apologizing, I told them about my new plan. I explained how I was going to have Ryan pick up our daughter and bring her down to Georgia so I could save up enough cash to move down there as well.

They were immediately concerned as Ryan had been deceitful and manipulative in the past, especially during the divorce process. They assumed he was up to something that would jeopardize my life and my daughter's life to benefit his own. It really was an ugly divorce, so I knew that they *could* be right, but at that point I had no choice but to gamble on his integrity.

As Ryan began his journey to Illinois to pick up our daughter, I started making the calls to set up auditions at topless clubs. I was convinced I had found my escape from my oppressive dependency on others. At least so I thought.

The Rod of Results

When I decided to become a stripper once again, I took my fierce loyalty to my child and set out to fix a financial problem. My intentions were good, and my mind ran on the fuel of frustration and disappointment to change my situation. I was tired of being the victim of a marital failure. I was sick of being the unwanted single mom whom most men were okay with sleeping with but none wanted to commit to. I was taking the accumulating pain and turning it into a vehicle of reaction just as I had done before. Only this time I wasn't looking to be accepted or esteemed by anyone whom I thought mattered; instead, I was taking my insecurities to the other side. A darker side. A side that made room for my frustration to manifest and lash out. I picked up my rod, threw it into my controversial situation, and demanded results!

You're probably wondering where this "rod" came from in my story. Well, let's just say it's a metaphor from the story of Moses, the man in the Bible who was called by God to lead the Israelites out of their slavery in Egypt and into a land God promised to them. The Israelites were a complaining people. Basically, their attitude sucked so badly it ended up taking them forty years to get somewhere that should have only taken a few days.

Moses spent *all* of these forty years leading them and dealing with their constant drama. One day they had come to a place on their journey that had absolutely no water to drink. The Israelites freaked out on Moses, and honestly, I can't blame them for panicking (I drink a gallon of water a day myself now), but God had already proven to them on countless occasions that he had their backs. He parted the Red Sea so that they could escape the Egyptians who were chasing them down. Their shoes never wore out, and food fell miraculously from the sky every morning. A giant cloud shaded them through each sun-scorching day, and a pillar of light illuminated their camp throughout each night. And yet once again they were hating on Moses and doubting God's provision. (see Exodus 32:25)

"What are *we* going to do?" they said (I'm paraphrasing). "Moses, *do* something!" they demanded. So, Moses asked God what he would have him do in this situation. And although God told him specifically only to speak to the rock, Moses was so frustrated by the griping people that he grabbed his rod and struck the stone rather than speak to it. Twice Moses did this, with fierce anger on his lips and in his swing. Suddenly water came pouring out of the rock, and the people cheered as they drank it up. It *worked*! Or so it seemed to Moses. The only problem with the result was, it wasn't done God's way. Moses allowed his anger and frustration to cause him to disobey God to get a result. Moses reacting to the people's frustration with his own frustration ended up costing him not only the chance of entering the promised land but also his life as well. Moses would die before the Israelites would step foot into the promise land that God had established for his people. His disobedience cost him everything!

I can't help but relate with Moses in this story as he certainly seemed to have the right to be frustrated. Who really cares *how* he executed the solution to the Israelites' problem as long as he was doing something to fix it, right?

I felt like it didn't matter how good I tried to be or how hard I tried to work; it never seemed to be enough. Enough to the ones who were on the sidelines judging me, the ones who were trying to protect me, or that voice inside me that said, "You have never been enough and you never will be enough."

When It Works . . .

The management at the first club I began working at after my divorce said they had never seen a girl hustle as hard as I did! I assigned myself to the confines of the smoky establishment from 2:00 p.m. to 2:00 a.m. six days a week. I completely engulfed myself in my mission. I rarely hung out with friends or went on dates. Instead, I was solely focused on accomplishing my financial goal. I was paying off bills, while buying things I never thought I could afford, and *still* managing to grow my savings account. "This is working!" I thought. Or at least it seemed to be.

But for how long? I mean, I never raised my hand in the second grade and said anything about being a stripper when I grew up!

The familiarity astounds me each time I chat with a girl now who is still in the industry, as that first conversation almost always invites the little girl inside her to engage. She tells me who she was meant to be. What she dreamt about being before she found herself here. Who she still plans on being one day. Hopefully. Maybe. It's as if the second-grade girl inside her is reaching up her hand and saying, "Hey! I'm still in here! I'm wearing this mask and these costumes, but underneath I'm still that girl who was going to be a veterinarian, a housewife, a missionary!"

As quickly as her childlike eyes light up, they grow dim just as fast explaining how life just became complicated. It became painful. It became desperate.

"What other choice do I have?" she says. She then catches a glimpse of herself in the mirror, and immediately the little girl vanishes as she adjusts her mask, slips back into her heels and into her self-preservation mode. She remembers the rejection she felt. Her fears. Her frustrations. As she grabs her rod, she grabs control and briefly possess all the answers, instant results, and a middle finger for all the backlash she will eventually receive from somewhere. She throws up her arm as she strikes the rock, not once but over and over again, each time killing a piece of the dream of who she once believed she could be and surrendering to the lie she believes she has become.

Chapter Six

Bible Belt Bad

I always wanted to be one of those incredibly strong people. You know, those people who never seem to bat an eye when faced with confrontation of any kind. Those people who couldn't and wouldn't be fazed by negative forces or intimidating circumstances designed to break their focus and self-confidence. Instead, they always seem to be in their element, regardless of what element they may find themselves in. I thought that if I could be more like "those people," then life couldn't get me. I wouldn't be swayed by emotions or paralyzed by insecurities or insufficiencies. I would stop being the victim of others' fickle emotions. Instead, *I* would be the one lacking empathy and sentiment in relationships.

But apparently that was *not* the way I was wired. I am a "feeler," which can be absolute chaos without restraint. I have felt my way through countless relationships, various jobs, and several impulsive undertakings. You may find me embarking on a new project one week to planning a new career the next to "Hey! I think I need a new puppy!"

While being a "feeler" might mean I'm extra compassionate and loyal to any number of different causes, it has also kept me emotionally invested in less than healthy situations that needed to be addressed from a more logical standpoint. Either way, I have found this characteristic to be a giant disadvantage in a society that seems to demand confrontation and the ability to compartmentalize.

When I decided to dance, I felt like I had finally turned off my sensitivity switch. I could be in control and completely detached from anyone. I was as close to being one of "those people" as I could be and commended myself on my bravery to do what I did. Of course, I completely altered my personality with the convenient numbing effects of alcohol. But I wasn't necessarily taking that factor into consideration. At least not right away. I was just glad to feel on top of my situation and my pesky emotions.

As my dancing days were coming to a close in Chicago, I couldn't help but think of Lot's wife in the story of Sodom and Gomorrah, the infamous wicked cities in the Bible that God chose to destroy. Lot, his wife, and children had to evacuate in order to avoid becoming part of the wreckage. Although God spared the lives of Lot and his family, there was only one stipulation to their survival: they could not look back! Of course, Lot's wife broke the one and only rule and immediately turned into a pillar of salt when she did (see Genesis 19).

When I heard this story as a kid, my eyes grew wide with the fatal outcome, and I was gripped with a rather fearful impression of God's unyielding punishment. I mean, what if she was just looking back because she heard the loud commotion of an entire city being swallowed up by fire and brimstone and her curiosity of such a catastrophic event got the best of her? What if it was just as simple as a fly buzzing around her head and she searched about her surroundings to swat it and her eyes accidently grazed the momentous scene? I felt like I wanted to defend Lot's wife's actions somehow, until I realized as an adult the real reason she was probably looking back.

Although she may have been caught grievously watching her name-brand clothes go up in smoke or her beautiful home crumble mercilessly to the ground, I now assume looking back was an instinctive physical response that exposed her true spiritual longing. Her heart was focused on what she was leaving behind instead of what God was calling her into. I also find it ironic she should turn into a pillar of salt. Was becoming something, we associate with thirst symbolic of the condition of one's soul when our eyes are not on Christ?

My short stint with dancing wasn't just a brief scandalous affair with the wild side of society anymore. Instead, it had become something that I knew. Something that I had become good at, until I even found myself wondering if I was qualified to do anything else. I had grown accustomed to throwing money around like it was air, and I was quickly finding my significance in the status of my financial liberties.

The last club I worked at in Chicago would prove to be the most bougie and maybe the most culpable of other suspicious activities. I don't know a whole lot about organized crime, but I couldn't help but notice the high-class, wealthy men who came in looking for girls to empty a whole bunch of money on. This was a far cry from the smoky, dated rock club I started in. this was a no-nonsense group of gentlemen who ran a high-class topless haven that did not tolerate any obnoxious stripper drama. If you so much as bickered with another dancer, you were immediately pulled into an office to be reprimanded by a stern face in a three-piece suit seated imperiously behind an intimidatingly massive desk.

The management was firm and uncompromising as it engaged with the dancers, much like an authoritarian father might use his dominant stature to subdue his child into compliance. I often wondered if this was the disciplinary method of choice, assuming most of these girls had some sort of issue with men, and maybe communicating with them the way a harsh father would was a sure way to keep them in line. The situation was odd, to say the least. Still, I enjoyed the strawberries and champagne and filet mignon with several customers during the course of each night I worked. No more bologna sandwiches made with love by a toothless house mom. Instead, the women hired to look after the dancers at this club were running a highly efficient factory for moneymakers, not an orphanage for lost girls with broken hearts and inevitable addictions.

I was feeling conflicted about my final exit out of stripping when I called a friend on my way to my last night at the club before my big move to Georgia. As soon as he answered, I began gushing to him about where I had been most of the day and who I was with. I explained to him that I was with a customer that I had met at the club. He had a legit bodyguard nearby the entire time I was with him, either following us around the mall or standing outside the door of the remote location of the house we later drove to. He told me because we had "hung out" that I had somehow been granted his protection. (Hmm . . . okay?)

I carried on to my friend about how gross and weird I thought this customer was, and the next thing I knew the same customer's voice emerged violently from the phone. His vocals startled me as they began belting through my Verizon network like a weapon, cursing me out and basically telling me how he was going to have me "whacked"! All the while, I just stared dumbfounded at my phone, wondering, "How did he hear me?" But mostly I was thinking," Oh my God! He is going to kill me!"

Terrified, I hung up on him and called my parents as if it were the last time I would hear their voices streaming through my tiny pink flip phone. As soon as one of them answered, I burst into tears as I tried to explain the "hit" on my life. Of course, they thought I was crazy. But this threat was enough to turn my head from the wicked cities burning up behind me and get back on the road in front of me. Well, I-75 south actually.

Unpleasant as it was to be threatened by a giant man you suspect to be part of some sort of mafia collaboration, I almost appreciated the final shove out of the clenches of the industry and into my packed-up vehicle headed straight down to Georgia. I had saved up enough money to get my own place, furnish it, and hopefully find a job to sustain me and my little family once I arrived. I had accomplished my financial mission, and I was ready to rededicate my life to Christ! As if that's how it works.

I drove through the majestic Blue Ridge Mountains listening to a Christian greatest hit CD from a few years back. It was all the Jesus paraphernalia I could scavenge from my parents' house, as I was attempting to prepare myself spiritually for the shiny new redemption plan I had waiting for me on the other side of these mountains. I was excited and optimistic about trying to unpeel my identity from "stripper Leah" with every mile that climbed on my odometer and faded out scenically in my rearview mirror.

My Jeep Liberty swerved tightly around the sharp curves of the breathtaking landscape as I sang along with the Australian accents of the Newsboys at the top of my lungs. I was having this incredible spiritual moment, coasting through God's stunning handiwork as I basked in the serenity of his presence. At one point in my journey I even attempted to memorize every word to "Stomp" by Kirk Franklin; its lyrics suddenly became the anthem and hype music for my upcoming Southern adventures.

I'm sure my performance was just as entertaining as it sounds. With my very white girl vocals trying to blend in with the likes of Kirk Franklin and his "GP" friends singing backup on the gospel track. I'm certain God got a little giggle out of it anyway.

This drive was a celebration. I had accomplished what I had set out to do financially, and I had survived! It was done. It was over. I was clocking out of my almost-three-month stint as a stripper, and I was ready to try doing this whole Christian lifestyle thing all over again. "I won't mess up this time," I told myself. "I won't react. I won't be moved by loneliness, anxiousness or desperation."

Little did I know I was driving into my own demise—on a road that would deliver me into every trigger and insecurity that I had been running from my entire life up until this point. My destination would be completely entangled in all the weeds that had overgrown and overtaken the very little hope I had left inside. I was in a new place, yes, but with the same misconception of God's love and the same toxic voice of the one I had just been granted a divorce from a few months prior.

I was initially thrilled to be driving into the land of God-fearing Christians, or the Bible Belt, as some would call it, as I really did desire to be surrounded by a culture that would support and celebrate my fragile faith. I pictured the harmonious nature of God's love radiating from the majority of the townspeople's faces and in their kind gestures. I assumed the Southern hospitality that I had only heard of would scoop me up and nestle me into its quiet community with care and acceptance. I couldn't have been more wrong in my preconception of what the Bible Belt really looked like.

While the aesthetics of *this* Southern town during this particular time were absolutely quaint and lovely, there was an unspoken law of segregation that one could not deny. It divided the blacks from the whites, the Hispanics from the blacks, the holy locals from the heathen locals, and of course the Northerners from the Southerners. It was disheartening, to say the least, to encounter some of the most judgmental Christians I had ever met on the town's street corners, who claimed to attend its church services on Sundays.

I also wasn't prepared to face the reality of who Ryan had become to me or the aggressive manipulation of his friends—the ones who used to be "our friends" and the very few people I knew in this faraway, foreign town. It didn't matter how much optimism or faith I had in my new element. Their brokenness was determined to find mine. And once it did, I simply lacked the confidence, cleverness, strength to withstand it. I had still not become one of "those people."

Shame was now snickering at me in every room I walked into. It dismantled my relevance in each conversation I found myself in. Landing a real job meant being me without alcohol to melt my anxieties away. It meant "pretending" to like myself or believe in myself long enough to convince someone else I was the right girl for the job. I was already on antidepressants and had been for the past couple years, but *nothing* could dissolve the tares that consumed me now. In fact, every voice I subscribed to seem only to fertilize them, feeding them whatever they needed to ensure their growth.

I also found it incredibly difficult to be alone when Ryan had his visitation time with Lily. It seemed when she was with me, I was complete, and when she wasn't, I was acutely aware of the gaping hole in my tarnished heart. Initially I would seek out relief and connection at random church events I found online. I even attended a couple of singles group meetings at a hip contemporary church in the area, only to find that its members' motives resembled the clichéd dynamics one might encounter at a bar (but without alcohol of course). I would later realize that I needed much more than a casual meeting at the local church or a little mixer with the singles group there. Instead, I was desperate for real, godly friends, a solid support group, and a divine understanding of who I really was in Christ.

What Choice Do I Have?

Ryan assured me he would do his best to help me get situated once I arrived in this place he had been calling home for at least a year now. I had no family, no resources, just the flimsy word of my ex-husband. I had yet to receive one child support payment upon arrival, and whenever I asked for it, he would try to pacify my request with some small cash here and there. My livelihood and that of my child seemed to be at the mercy of his meager generosity.

I threatened to move back to Illinois, as our child custody arrangement was still there and I assumed I could get the state to intervene where his promises fell short. My frustration grew with his dishonesty and my desperation. Each time I would threaten to leave, he and his girlfriend would show up at my door with a bag of cheap food, such as hot dogs or bologna, while Lily and I stood dispirited behind the thick tension that hung bitterly on their haughty faces. Their eyes peered down in disgust at my presence, then roamed disapprovingly around the shell of the apartment we were now calling home. I didn't want their hot dogs or their approval of my living room furniture! I just wanted a child support payment and to be treated like a human being when exchanging our child. I immediately regretted my move to Mapleview, and my parents' reservations about the risky decision began ringing painfully in my humbled ears.

The money I drove down to Georgia with was being spent in Georgia fast. Although I did find a salon to work in, I had to pay booth rent, which was kind of hard to do without any clientele whatsoever. Then, of course, there was child care, utilities, a car payment, insurance, etc. I began doing random jobs for the few people I'd met since my arrival, like cleaning houses or doing in-home highlights or haircuts, but that was clearly not enough to live on.

So, I looked at God, then I looked at my child, and said to myself, "What choice do I have?" I'd like to say this was a moment of defeat and surrender, but it wasn't. It was a defining moment of false self-empowerment. I was going to become "her" again. As long as I was "her," they couldn't hurt me. It seemed everyone was going to judge and criticize me no matter what I did, so I figured I might as well have money and a twisted sense of power to boot. Adrenaline raced through my blood as I changed direction. I put on the mask, slipped on the shoes, grabbed my rod, and began stripping in Mapleview, Georgia.

But something was different in this new little town. Actually, many things were different. I wasn't hiding in the bright lights and forgiving streets of the big city anymore. Instead, I was bending over to receive a legalistic spanking as the sting of the Bible Belt swung hard in a small town and especially on sinners like me. I went from feeling like a controversial sex goddess in the big city to a white trash whore in a small Southern town.

Suddenly all of my pain was cornering me at once: my failure at marriage, my inability to provide a decent living for my child, my many experiences with rejection, and repeated condemnation from Christians. It was like an avalanche of fiery darts that my soul was much too brittle to withstand. I felt myself becoming the death of their words and the product of their unrelenting shame. After retreating back to Illinois with Lily for over a month shortly after moving away, Ryan's apologies and persuasive promises eventually convinced me to return to the Southern town once again.

5 Months Later . . .

I became really close to the three guys that lived together in the apartment across from mine. We shared a balcony, a cable wire and the same social outcast stigma associated with our lack of accomplishment or direction in life. Mark was a friend of theirs before I had ever met him. He arrived on my tragic scene just as everyone else in it began to retreat. The night I seduced him was the same night I threw my next-door neighbors coffee pot on the ground after arguing with him about who was responsible for breaking my DVD player. I picked up a spatula and began beating the kitchen appliance as violent tears broke from every hopeless place inside of me.

"I hate you! I hate you! I hate you!" I shouted at my neighbors, as I simultaneously destroyed the kitchenware. But really, I hated *me* and what I had become.

Mark had arrived just a few minutes after my neurotic episode with the neighbors. I approached him like a hunter approaches his prey; I was on an aggressive pursuit to feed my addiction. I was spiritually and emotionally famished, and ambushing someone sexually was an attempt simply to survive. Like a vampire feeds on the blood of its innocent victims, I fed on the sexual submission of men. I needed to lure someone in and succeed in the claiming of his full attention. Only then could I let go of everything gripping me, leaving me, or rejecting my love—my devious intent hidden behind a sultry facade. I was like a junky concealing the evidence of her chemical crutch; only the evidence of *my* addiction did not hide beneath long-sleeved shirts, or makeup. Instead my dirty habit was masked by a phony self-confidence and fabricated desire for my prey. As I sprinkled his ears with what he longed to hear, I basted his pride with everything he desired to feel, boiled and simmered an image he longed to behold, then licked my lips, grabbed a fork, and began to indulge on my spiritual supper.

I had reacted to each dilemma or broken heart frivolously. Like the desperate efforts of a gambler dealt numerous losing hands, I had finally thrown down the very little I had left on the only man still interested in even having me. Mark was not a guy I would have been typically drawn to, yet his voice was ever so calming in the most horrific hours of a most violent storm. His gentle demeanor soothed the chaos that gripped my nerves and paralyzed my spirit. He swept into my life out of nowhere and slipped out of it just as mysteriously.

Chapter Seven

Pink Elephants

Mark and I had only been dating for maybe a week or two when he made his way over to my apartment one afternoon. I had already been sipping on White Zinfandel for at least a couple hours. I wasn't looking to get drunk from alcohol; I was looking to avoid getting sick from *not* drinking alcohol. Who knew this is how alcoholism worked? Not me!

I had only known a couple people whom others would consider "alcoholics," and I assumed these were people who woke up every day and drank because, well, they wanted to. I had no idea how their body would respond once they abruptly stopped drinking. "How could one be addicted to alcohol?" I thought. It's not like heroin or cocaine. To me alcohol was the safest substance to abuse since it was legal, first of all, and second, it wasn't physically addictive. Or so I thought.

Soon after Mark arrived, my throat began to burn more with each sip of the cold pink wine. I tried to continue to drink it anyway, but it literally felt like someone was holding a burning match up to my tonsils.

"I must be getting sick," I said as I held my throat, somewhat perplexed by how rapidly the pain was increasing. I put my glass down and decided to take a bath to soothe the aches and chills I was experiencing. When I slipped into the warm water, my limbs began to tremble uncontrollably. Now, "the shakes" were nothing new to me, as I had experienced them on several occasions over the past several months. What confused me about this time, however, was the fact that I had alcohol in my system. I mean, I had been sipping on wine *all* day.

Mark began pouring the bath water down my back as it seemed to ease the intensity of my discomfort.

"What's going on with you?" he asked kindly as he watched my trembling form flailing relentlessly in the bathtub.

"I always shake when I stop drinking. That's why I hate dancing," I explained. "I have to drink so much to do it, and this is what happens when I stop."

"You poor thing," he said in a sympathetic tone as he watched the cruel effects of alcohol withdrawal begin to ravage my limbs and hijack my nervous system. He then began to examine the bruises splattered randomly across my shaky legs; they were from the floor tricks I attempted to do on the stage. I kind of laughed as I explained those, but his gaze seemed only to grieve my condition, as he replied, "Look what this job has done to your body." His words were as calming and medicating as the warm water he was committed to pouring down my back. But they also forced me to confront the reality of what working in this environment *was* doing to my body! The fact that I was detoxing in front of someone else for the first time was pretty confrontational all on its own.

I just shrugged my shoulders like a true soldier as if to say, "Yup, comes with the job I suppose."

I assumed this would be the worst of it, and I would just have Mark there with me to hang on to for the miserable ride. A ride I felt I could predict by this point. I was going to shake, feel sick, sweat, get a little paranoid, and maybe have some nightmares. I was hoping that if I was in fact sick, maybe this "bug" would help knock me out and I could sleep through the worst of it. But I could never prepare myself nor remotely predict what was in store for me that night.

Pink Elephants on Parade

If you have ever seen the Disney movie *Dumbo*, then you will know exactly what I'm talking about here. There is a scene in the movie where Dumbo, the freakishly large-eared elephant, accidentally drinks moonshine with his little circus mouse friend, and they end up getting completely hammered. They both begin staggering around, with the occasional hiccup and goofy grin, as they mimic the classic drunken behavior of humans. But what happens next in the film is what kept me up at night as a little kid.

Things take a psychedelic turn when Dumbo blows a massive bubble with his trunk and it turns into a giant pink elephant! Suddenly there are several giant pink elephants with evil eyes emerging from every corner of the screen singing, "Look out! Look out! Pink elephants on parade!" The song goes on, and the elephants just get scarier and weirder as the scene unfolds. As a kid I had no idea what was happening here; I just knew it scared the living heebie-jeebies out of me! As I got older, I would learn what Dumbo and his friend were experiencing was actually associated with delirium tremens, which is also loosely referred to as "pink elephants" and described as hallucinations caused by alcohol or alcohol withdrawal.

My apartment walls were adorned with black-and-white portraits of Marilyn Monroe, Audrey Hepburn, and other vintage models and actresses from the 1960s era. The paint color was a violet pink that swallowed up the living room drywall and reflected its girly hue into the crystal chandelier hanging in the small boutique-style room. My decor was a middle finger to the idea of ever sharing a living space with a man again. I purposely chose black pleather couches with cushions that were wrapped in tan leopard-print upholstery to complete a very "this is my place, not yours" kind of look.

My Pink Elephants

I could hardly climb out of the bathtub, as my legs at this point had become like wiggly stilts made of jelly.

"Oh my God! I can't walk!" I cried. Panic began to set in as my neighbor friends who had arrived shortly before my bath, emerged from the living room to see what was going on. "I feel sick!" I said. "I think I need some fresh air!" Two of the guys helped Mark as they wrapped a small blanket around my wet body, trying to grab hold of one of my trembling limbs to pick me up and carry me outside. Once they got me into the night air, they quickly realized they would need to carry me right back inside, as the scene was drawing attention from the other neighbors in my apartment building.

All three of them, wide eyed with panic, had just smoked some weed right before my alcohol-induced breakdown. They looked at each other with glassy eyes and maybe a tad bit of paranoia.

"What do we do with her?" one said to another as they grudgingly held up my crippling body like a piece of evidence they needed to dispose of *and fast*. They carried me back into the apartment and placed me on the long leopard-print couch.

My body began clenching up periodically as if I were having seizures. My jaw clenched as my teeth grinded against each other with each violent pull of my neck and spine. One of my friends finally phoned the hospital and asked someone what they should do with me. The hospital apparently told him that the ER would probably scare me at this point since the hallucinations had already begun. They suggested that I just stay home and ride it out.

I had no idea how deadly it could be to detox from alcohol, not to mention the antidepressants I had abruptly quit taking a week or so prior to this incident. But I was determined to stay sane and keep all of my teeth, so I had my friends find something for me to bite down on through each seizure-like episode. Mark held down my thrashing legs and gave me small sips of water since I couldn't hold anything myself. I was unbearably thirsty, but each time I tried to drink more than a sip, I would immediately begin vomiting everything I had just taken in and more.

As I sat miserably in my living room, only faintly aware of my friends coming in and out of my apartment, I started to notice something strangely peculiar. The pictures on my living room walls had souls. Evil souls. I looked up at them, then quickly looked away as their eyes glared sharply into mine and their smiles coiled up into their distorted faces. Each one taunted me as if issuing an impending doom on my life.

These were anything *but* "pink elephants" emerging from my apartment walls! Who knew Marilyn Monroe could morph into the devil himself?! And Audrey Hepburn's eyes became black holes that swallowed my sanity until eventually I had nowhere to look but down. Even the faces of my friends transformed into terrifying demonic entities. I stared at the floor holding on to reality for dear life as an emptiness began to settle into my bones.

I was used to praying when I detoxed from alcohol in the past, immediately experiencing a sense of comfort or relief from the fear. Even if it was just for a moment. One of my neighbor friends, who had also grown up in church, was sitting on the couch next to me when I leaned over to him and confessed with tears welling up in my eyes, "God is gone! I'm praying to him, but I can't feel him anymore. He's sick of me doing this crap, and he's not bothering with me anymore."

He laid his head down next to mine as he attempted to assure me, "God is not gone, Leah. He still hears you."

"But I've never felt this absence before!" I tried to explain in defeat. "This is different." There was a long pause as I grieved what I perceived as God's rejection. "Will you pray for me?" I asked humbly, looking up into his glassy pink eyes.

"Of course, I will." He put his hand on my shoulder and prayed a nice sweet prayer. I can't remember at all what he said. All I can remember was thinking how wimpy the prayer was. "Doesn't this guy realize I need some Holy Ghost intercession up in here! My life is on the line, and you're praying your safe little nursery rhyme?!"

I felt completely alone. My living room seemed to weigh over me as if the utter despair I was sitting in were tangible. No God. No hope. Just the terror and taunting of evil spirits circling my soul. It was as if I were somewhere between earth and hell and a clan of demons were just having a pre party with my sanity and bodily functions before they threw me over their shoulders and dragged me into the eternal flames of hell.

Suddenly my nose started bleeding profusely, but I was trembling so hard I couldn't control the blood from making its way down my throat. I began choking and gasping for air. I assume the guys had gone outside to smoke as I found myself alone during the moment I probably needed them the most. A deep sense of dread struck me, and I thought to myself, "Oh my God! This is it! This is how I die!" Buck naked in a floral throw blanket with three friends outside somewhere, probably too high to save me even if they found me in time. Suddenly I was able to swallow the stream of blood dripping down my throat, then breathed in all the precious air my lungs could possibly fill themselves with.

As the night dragged on, I kept asking my friends, "How long will this last? Does anyone know?" Mark proceeded to research my predicament online, only to inform me these hallucinations could last for *days*! Now, I have done my share of hallucinogenic drugs, and believe me when I say, there were times I couldn't wait for the trip to end. However, I also had a good idea of *when* the trip would end. But *days*?! He began to explain how the receptors in my brain were hypersensitive because they had adapted to the desensitizing effects of the alcohol and blah-blah-blah. As he carried on, I just sat there envisioning my brain short-circuiting into absolute chaos and lunacy. "What have I done to my poor brain!" I thought.

As the dawn began to seep through the cracks of my living room blinds, relief began to seep into my body and into my crazy head as well. I was completely exhausted, which actually felt nice as I could finally relax a bit. I was still naked and covered in blood, puke, and my tiny blanket of course. Yet inside I was secretly celebrating my survival of the night of horrors. I was still alive! I was given a second chance! I felt God's grace like a giant life preserver, pulling my body out of the violent waves of death and into the remission of the shoreline.

Mark had left for work, and one of my neighbor friends (who would ironically die of alcoholism years later) stayed at my place to keep an eye on me. He sat down then stretched himself out on the couch across from mine, after finding the Christian music channel for me on the TV. A song called "In the Light" started to play through the television speakers and automatically filled the room with a sense of restoration. The lyrics to the song rang like angel kisses in my ears, as I literally felt as though I had just survived a portion of hell. I stared into the TV at the pictures of the Christian music group dc Talk being displayed across the screen. When this song came out, I thought I was way too cool for these "Christian" bands, and although this song had a ring to it, I was too busy sulking to the sounds of Tori Amos and Nine Inch Nails when this album came out.

But the nostalgia of this song embraced me. Like the sound of my mom's voice ringing from the kitchen at dinnertime, or the predictable thump the front door made when my dad got home from work at night. This song was home. Its message was what I knew and what I grew up on regardless of how far I tried to run away from its influence. I couldn't have appreciated my Christian upbringing any more than I did in that moment, as I was drawn to the glow of the screen like a flower bending into the sunlight.

This horrific night made it clear to me that I had to figure something else out and *fast*. I began filling out applications all over town for mostly minimum wage jobs. I was desperate for anything, but it became evident the places I went to look for a job were not as desperate for me.

It was difficult enough to walk away from the easy, yet not-so-easy, money that comes from dancing to work an honest job. But the rejection from these minimum wage companies was just too much. Bills were piling up once again along with my insecurities that had become dependent on stripping, just as my body had become dependent on alcohol to feel normal. I couldn't go back home to Illinois, as my pride stood rightfully by my horrible decisions. As if I needed another "I told you so" from anyone. Instead, I wearily picked up my rod, placed my head back into the yoke, only this time with the looming fear of returning to my own hellish pink elephants

experience.

Chapter Eight

To Lose a Life

For whoever wants to save their life will lose it, but

whoever loses their life for me will find it.

(Matthew 16:25 NIV)

Autumn began to wither up all around me as the

November chill breathed a deadly cold into the trees. My

eyes stared blankly into a cool breeze that gently played

with my hair and rustled through the crisp, crackling

leaves. The tranquil sounds breathing through the air

composed a bittersweet melody that seemed to serenade my

farewell to each failed attempt I had made at life. I spent

each day that my daughter was at her fathers on the cement

balcony of my apartment building, sipping from a

bottomless cup of cheap red wine, between long drags of

endless cigarettes. The peaceful solitude seemed to bewitch

me, and I was being drawn into the serenity of a death that

was swallowing not only my purpose in living but the sounds of life that once surrounded me as well.

The graceful exit of the departing season seemed to validate the desperate petition being made inside my head. There was a small but convincing voice that grew stronger and gained more dominion over my thoughts with each passing day. The idea of taking my own life became a quite reasonable and almost a harmonious alternative to living in a broken world with its inevitable heartache. Besides, a world without me in it began making a lot more sense, as I felt my existence now only polluted an otherwise functional society. One made up of people capable of managing the pressures while balancing various roles in life. It seemed everyone everywhere understood something that I couldn't quite grasp. They stood with esteem against any opposition, clever and collected in their successes. And there I was, feeling too incompetent even to leave my porch.

Confessions

I believe one of the bravest moments we can have is the moment we can admit that we are simply not okay. It's a pivotal instant that commands the chaos of our recklessness and confusion to be subdued to our convictions. It removes all the masks we've tried on or worn out and allows us to be seen. It turns on a light that begins to remove the darkness that once swallowed up our entire perception. We make a liberating confession into the atmosphere that calls for something bigger and stronger to sweep in and catch us just before we plummet into the earth. The stress of trying to find places to hide it and the taxing burden of trying to bandage it before it bleeds out are ultimately exposed. We can finally throw up our arms and say, "Here it is, all of it! I'm still in it! I still have its residue on my hands, and the taste of it is still in my mouth! I'm not even sure where the exit sign is to get out of it! But this is where I am."

Going to God Dirty

All my life I was under the impression that you had to turn your life around before you could have a relationship with God. I thought you had to clean yourself up before God could clean you up. It makes zero sense, I know. I wondered, "How could someone walk with God and walk him directly into their sin?" I was certain that some sins just completely freaked him out! I mean, if he actually saw where I was and what I was doing there, he would be *shocked* and absolutely repulsed because *surely* it would be the worst thing he has ever seen!

So, I convinced myself that once I quit dancing, *then* I could quit drinking. And once I quit the two of those, *then* I could recommit my life to Christ. But until *then*, I had to figure this whole life thing out on my own.

My idea of being a Christian was obviously very performance based. When I was serving God, I was constantly beating myself up for letting him down somehow. Or I just compared myself to other people who looked or acted more Christian than myself. I certainly didn't look like anyone I had ever seen in a church calling themselves a Christian, especially now that I was residing in the strongly conservative South where the heavy glances hit almost as hard as the fire and brimstone that poured out of their megaphones on any given Sunday afternoon.

Time seemed to brand me the town trash with each day that I seemed to be stuck in. My once high-energy and health-conscious self-faded rapidly as my organs felt like they were just puttering along through each day of abuse. Every bill that came up or strong desire I had to splurge on something expensive to feel valuable seemed to whisper into my consciousness, "You're never getting out of this."

Sometimes I would just stare at my daughter in defeat, as my heart sank with my lack of options. "How are we ever going to make it on our own if I'm not stripping?"

I thought. This was supposed to be about *us*! This gig was supposed to be an opportunity to move forward with our lives! What I was finding at the end of this seemingly harmless shortcut was a big black hole that swallowed even my best of intentions, leaving me enslaved to a new distorted perception of myself —a price much higher than any rent payment or car note. When I couldn't see the end in sight, a great weight of hopelessness settled into my bones. I was convinced that if all the alcohol I was consuming didn't kill me, then the state of mind I was in certainly would.

The more aware I was of my own defeat in the battle over controlling my own life, the more I began verbally swinging at everyone who I felt had wronged me along the way. I would call my dad and ream him out over all the times he had let me down. Initially, he would argue his case and defend himself against my pointed words, but then one day he stopped fighting back. Later he told me how the Holy Spirit spoke to him and urged him to stop and just listen to me. God had told my father that I simply had a broken heart.

When I felt like my family could hear my pain, I began to confide in them about how I was trying to medicate it. They quickly became a small light that I could depend on to guide me home regardless of my condition. This made it possible for me to open up to them about the reality of my struggle. Instead of rebuking me, they began praying for me over the phone and calling me just to tell me they loved me. Because they were showing me love and grace in the middle of my mess, the door was swung wide open for me to believe that God could do the same.

In the past I would feel bad and repent of my sins, only to find myself walking right back into the very things I was repenting of! I felt like such a hypocrite with God that I wasn't even sure what to say to him one particular time. "Certainly, he won't believe me," I thought. I wasn't even sure if I could believe myself! Yet this time was different. Instead of questioning my own motives and words with God, I had a super honest talk with him that didn't involve me making a bunch of promises that I wasn't sure I could keep. I didn't assure him that I would never strip again; I didn't do anything radical like ignite a bonfire to destroy all my secular paraphernalia. I just asked him to help me, to change me.

The very next night I drove to the strip club listening to praise and worship music and singing along at the top of my lungs. I wasn't trying to tune out the Holy Spirit anymore; instead, I welcomed his voice. I became transparent with God, my family, and finally myself about what I was really dealing with. God met me in my dark place, took my hand, and gently guided me into the light. If I didn't have the strength to step away from my issues, then I was going to bring him into them with me!

When I walked into work that night, I had this incredible peace. It almost felt like a soft, fuzzy blanket that wrapped around my shoulders and warmed me from the inside out. I even hesitated to start ordering drinks upon arrival as I usually did to get into my "I've got this" zone. This feeling was so amazing that I didn't want to ruin it with any outside substance. I just wanted to be swaddled in it for the rest of my life! But as I started roaming about the club, I began viewing the entire scene through a completely different set of eyes. It was as if God had poked a hole through the atmosphere and said, "Take a look through here and see what I see."

My eyes began to probe a room where up until this moment I had only seen the money I could make or catty drunk girls I needed to avoid. Only now a curtain was pulled back with my gaze transfixed on a display of lost souls. My spirit was moved by a room full of broken, empty individuals, each trying to fill the other with a value that would leak out of them before they could ever be filled. I was experiencing a very clear vision of what was *actually* happening in the room. With me. With them. With all of us!

However powerful this whole moment of spiritually heightened awareness was, I still thought, "Okay, show's over! I need to get back to business as usual, make some money!" I began tipping back drinks with an anticipation of a buzz to kick in that never did. In fact, the whole "warm and fuzzy" God sensation was still very prevalent over me, as if it refused to be drowned out by alcohol. I couldn't take it anymore; I *had* to tell someone. I ran into the bathroom and called a friend of mine.

"The strangest thing is happening!" I said. "God was showing me all this crazy stuff and now I can't get drunk!"

He replied, "Huh? That's crazy!" Especially after I named off all the alcoholic beverages I had just consumed.

I was completely floored by what was happening! I found myself sitting in the dressing room talking to the other dancers about how much God loves us and how he has an amazing plan and purpose for our lives. Oddly enough, they seemed to have needed to hear this good news as much as I did! There was a root of rejection in all of us that could never be resolved regardless of how much money or attention we received. I began to wonder, if we really had a clear revelation of God's love for us, would this lifestyle really have anything to offer us anymore?

Surrender

The more I saw myself as a child of God, the less I identified myself by my sin and failures. When I finally walked away from dancing, I stepped away as a girl still crippled but ready to hobble her way into the arms of her Savior. I was determined to know who *"I was* in Christ! I needed a relationship with him that wasn't dependent on the flailing emotions or inevitable disapproval of other people.

To save my life I would need to let go of the idea that I could rely on my own understanding to live it. I would have to forfeit my own perception of who I was and what I could be to a God who loves me and gave himself for me. In surrendering myself to Christ I would find my joy, my peace, my freedom, and finally my *life*.

Chapter Nine

Severed

Christmas was still a couple weeks away, but I simply couldn't wait that long to see her in it. I zipped her up into the leopard-print holiday dress made with fabric that felt soft and dense like corduroy. Its hemline was sweetly adorned with a red velvet ribbon that also wrapped perfectly around her three-year-old waist. She smiled and giggled as I curled her light brown hair and pinned it up into a formal style, suitable for a princess. She always loved getting dressed up, her excitement exceeding her brightly lit smile and running wild through her small, energy-infused legs. She raced back and forth across the balcony and into the living room during our ongoing little game of Simon Says. I would begin with, "Simon says, pat your head," and immediately she would tremble with giggles as she patted her head and anticipated the next assignment. "Simon says, bat your eyes." Her tiny little eyelashes would flutter as quickly as eyelashes can "Now stomp your feet," I concluded. Without hesitation her shiny black Mary Janes hit the floor while a mischievous grin spread across her face, and together we would sing, "Simon didn't say!"

I had already begun to pack up our things as I intended to move us back to Illinois before the holidays. I had officially quit dancing, and holding myself hostage to a lifestyle and an environment that was only deteriorating my soul. My eyes were now capable of peeking through the thick tares that had been blinding me, and my head was slowly slipping out of the heavy yoke, each day bringing me closer to my escape out of my debilitating situation. Whatever life I had established in Mapleview had already packed itself up into a tidy compartment of past tense, and my heart began to disconnect with the ones whom I would be bidding an unapologetic good-bye.

I had come to myself, much like the awakening experience described in the parable of the prodigal son. When the wayward young man found himself so hungry that pig slop started to look just as mouthwatering as chocolate cake, he was like, "What the heck is wrong with me? Have I become this desperate and hungry that just about anything looks good? Have I lost all confidence and self-worth that I've subjected myself to a life with far worse living conditions than the pigs I've been hired to care for?"

The thing was, like the prodigal son I knew a different life. This was actually a foreign land to me. I had been taught right from wrong and good from evil. I had spiritual discernment and a moral compass. Perhaps even the best of intentions can be swallowed up in the unrelenting tares or driven out into the despair of darkness, lost to one's own unbearable thirst.

The Bible says that the prodigal's father had servants and plenty of livestock, which leaves me with the impression that the place his son ran away from was not all that bad. He was fed, he was clothed, *and* he had servants. I can't help but wonder why he felt as though he needed to stray from such a place. Was it his curiosity that sent him out into a foreign land to squander all of his money and morality? Did he struggle with identity? Did he feel misunderstood? The main principle here is that there is always a *why* to the *what*. I mean, he was basically paying people to party with him and for chicks to have sex with him. What kind of tares had grown up and around his perspective of himself and his father that he couldn't see the destructive trap he was walking right into?

When the Bible states of the prodigal son, "he came to himself," I believe it means he instantly saw the trap for what it was and he was immediately willing to do whatever it took to make things right with his father again (Luke

15:17 NKJV). He had seen for himself how quickly momentary pleasures dissipate from one's hands and evaporate from an ever-longing soul. At last his value wasn't tied up in what he had or how others viewed him. Rather, his worth was now pending on the reconciliation of his father's love. He wasn't in a perpetual "give me" mode anymore. The one that insisted he feed the famished beast crying out mercilessly from within for validation and instant gratification. Instead, he finally understood that his best life was actually at the humble center of a servant's heart. His cry had gone from "give me what I want" to "make me who you want me to be" as his soul passion was now to serve his father.

I had come to a place where the "stuff" didn't matter. The status didn't matter, and the independence didn't either. I realized that it was my pride that kept me groveling with the pigs. That and the commitment I had to serving my flesh and proving everyone else wrong. But now I was standing up for myself and my little girl by surrendering to God and trusting his way even if it didn't include everything I thought it was supposed to. I realized that surrender meant I couldn't get frustrated and pick up my rod and start swinging it at my situation every time I felt some sort of injustice, insecurity, or offense. Instead, I would draw my justice, affirmation, and joy from a new source. One that neither I nor my circumstances could control. Rather, I would plunge my empty bucket into the unwavering, unrelenting, all-sufficient presence of God and be filled in ways that are simply not possible on my own.

A Mother's Worst Nightmare

Ryan had called me earlier one evening to see if Lily could join their family for a birthday party. Although I found it odd they were celebrating a birthday on a Wednesday night, I agreed to his request as I figured it would be fun for Lily and an opportunity for her dad to spend time with her before we left.

When Ryan arrived at my apartment to pick up Lily, I dotingly straightened her dress and adjusted the red bow neatly nestled in her curls before he scooped her up into his arms.

"So, just a couple hours, right?" I asked, my gaze urging his for an honest answer.

"Yeah, just a couple hours," he responded faintly as he nodded his head and cast his eyes anywhere but toward mine. He stood there for what seemed like forever, considering how quickly these exchanges had been over the past few weeks.

"Hey, you've got to see these pictures I just took of Lily!" I said as I gleamed, reaching for my hot pink digital camera. I began to scroll proudly through the photos of a delighted little girl cradling the small gray kitten we had just adopted. "Isn't this one absolutely adorable?" I continued, gloating over the cuteness of our little girl in her Christmas dress.

Just a few weeks before this particular night, I had dressed her up in a sequin top of mine that fit her much like a chic tube-style dress one would parade in along the red carpet. I had wrapped a feather boa around her neck and lined her small lips with a bright, cherry red lipstick. She looked like a movie star straight out of the Roaring Twenties. I was so impressed with how they turned out that I posted them on my Myspace account along with several other creative photo ideas I had come up with. Other photo shoots included her many Disney princess costumes, a silly impression of an '80s rock star, and of course a sweet pink ballerina leotard complete with tiny ballet slippers—all of which I invited her dad to see, as I assumed he would enjoy viewing them as much as we had enjoyed taking them.

As I continued to scroll from one picture to the next, I soon realized I was the only one interested in viewing the images on the digital screen. As I nudged him with my excitement to view another picture, he responded, "Yeah, yeah, I see," his voice batting me away with annoyance as his eyes strangely avoided me and the camera full of adorable pictures. He stood there another minute examining Lily in a way I had never seen before. He seemed emotional yet sheepish. I couldn't tell if he was flooded with sentiment or sadness, but either way his precarious behavior left me feeling suspicious and unsettled.

As he finally began to make his way from the balcony of my apartment to the stairs, I yelled out, "Bye, Chubby Choo!" (her nickname as a baby). "See you later!" I sang, waving enthusiastically over the wooden railing and into the night sky. She waved back, saying, "Bye, Mommy!" with her tiny little voice, and I watched him carry her off into the darkness of the chilly December night.

The significance of this moment could not have been foreseen, but it's a moment I will replay in my mind with a crippling regret for the rest of my life. It was the very last moment I would share with my little girl, at least in the way we had always known. The knives were being sharpened; the devious planning was underway. All I knew was, he was taking her to a birthday party, but there was never *really* a birthday party.

I felt a strange sense of doom come over me as his car pulled away and navigated slowly out the entrance of my apartment complex. As Mark and I proceeded to head out that night to grab some dinner, I struggled to shake the daunting "bad feeling" that nagged persistently at my better judgment. I called Ryan not even an hour after I saw him, hoping to disarm my suspicions and move on with my night. Each ring that went unanswered seem to confirm my God-given instinct and caused my blood to run a sharp cold beneath my skin.

After several unanswered calls he would finally respond, but with a different sound in his voice than I had heard in some time. It had a presumptuous tone, one that challenged its opponent to a battle of supremacy. It was smoothe and sly and riddled with cruel games as he told me he was not bringing Lily home. If I could have roared like a fierce lion in response to his goading, I certainly would have. Instead, I just turned into a crazed mom, as if steam poured out of my ears, curse words barreling defiantly out of my mouth. Everything inside me was jumping through that phone like a pit bull on an unannounced intruder. Yet he only seemed amused by my hysteria, like an evil villain who's gained power over his target. My fighting words flew at him like pebbles, barely clipping Goliath's toenails. By the time I hung up the phone, I was furious but not defeated, and I quickly drove home to scoop up my court order and take it directly to the police station. Surely, they would read our custody agreement and put an end to this psychotic game my ex was playing with our little girl.

I stormed into the police station like any determined mother in hot pursuit to retrieve her own flesh and blood. I immediately began making my case to the police officer there, confident he would see the order and recover my child as soon as possible. Instead, he looked at me sideways, and with an excruciatingly thick Southern drawl he said, "Now, this here, this is an Illinois order. I don't know what none of this even means." He continued, "This could be his visitation time for all I know. You're gonna have to wait a couple weeks till we can step in and do anything." He smirked. Having only casually skimmed over the order, he had made up his mind he was not going to acknowledge it, let alone act on it. Panic began to gnaw at my bones as I realized I was speaking to a cop who may have just as well been one of the demented characters in the 1972 thriller *Deliverance*.

"Are you still driving around here with an Illinois driver's license?" he asked, diverting the conversation from the abduction of my child by her father to a legal violation of mine.

"What?" I responded with frustration and disbelief. "Yes, but it's a valid driver's license and I haven't even lived here consistently for six months! Everything I have is still registered in Illinois, including my court order which states I have full custody of a child that my ex-husband is holding captive somewhere!"

"Well now." His eyes reached down into mine as if to corner me in my own complaint, like a child being reprimanded for tattling. "I can give you a ticket for driving around with a Illinois driver's license in the state of Georgia." His extremely slow speech and arrogant stare only provoked my intense plea for urgency and call to action, until I realized exactly what he was doing.

Suddenly every creepy movie I had ever watched that was based on a community of crooked, psychopathic people running a small town came back to haunt me. You know, the ones where the main character just happens to stumble upon an unknown, unheard-of location while on their way to somewhere else? Usually their car breaks down or the interstate is closed, and they find themselves in a quiet little town where its peculiar goings-on are quite possibly a threat to their very life! When the visitor tries to leave the suspected town of horrors, their desperate efforts collide with the crushing reality that they won't be going anywhere. All hope collapses into harrowing defeat as their getaway vehicle is cornered by the general store owner, the mailman, and of course the sheriff of the corrupt community.

Without any cooperation from the police, I was on my own in trying to figure out how to bring my daughter back into my arms. I may not have been able to get anywhere with anyone in Georgia, but I thought surely someone in Illinois will intervene and save the day! When I had finally gotten a hold of the woman assigned to our custody arrangement in my home state, I was completely bewildered by her lack of regard for the whole matter. She was rather rude and dismissive as I attempted to gain her assistance in my crisis. It seemed she was already anticipating my call and had already formed an unwarranted opinion of me and my situation. It was as if she had drunk the same Kool-Aid as everyone else in the uncooperative town. Had Ryan really thought of everything? My head began to spin in the madness of it all. It was as though my ex-husband had covered all his bases, as everyone I went to for help seemed to be stonewalling me. Had he convinced everyone to buy into some elaborate version of our story? One that solely served to execute his ingenious plan to obtain power and revenge by severing from me what I cared about most: my little girl.

The Cut

Less than 48 hours had passed since Lily had disappeared into her father's care. I spent each moment of her absence immersed in my mission of bringing her home until Friday came and suddenly there was a knock on my door. My heart stopped at the initial firm thump that broke the grave silence inside my apartment walls. When I opened the door, the nightmare continued to unfold as two well-dressed men stood militantly at my door. The looks on their faces told me right away they were definitely not there on my behalf. They looked as if they were about to strap me down to a lie detector test and interrogate me about a massive drug operation going on in my apartment building.

"Are you Leah Peppard?" one of the men asked sternly.

"Yes I am," I answered, confused, as my whole body began to crumble under the heavy weight and authority in his voice.

"May we have a look around?" the other one inquired, as they had already begun making their way through the door. Their probing eyes initiated the investigation; then they began peeking into shopping bags and shuffling through the paperwork on my kitchen table.

"What's going on?" I asked. I felt the color in my face rival the dingy shade of white painted across the popcorn ceiling of my tiny home. They looked at me with a combination of disgust and tyranny as one of them informed me that the pictures I had posted of my daughter on Myspace were reported as sexually explicit and needed to be removed from the site immediately. The whole moment felt like an out-of-body experience. First of all, I would never exhibit my child in a sexual way, ever! Anywhere! But at this point I literally agreed to do whatever they said as if my life and the life of my child were dependent on it. Suddenly all the precarious events leading up to this moment quickly went from circumstances one might only observe from their couch or a paid, plush seat in the movie theater to actual real life! The two men left after they were satisfied with their brief investigation of my home but as I closed the door behind them, I sensed that my predicament was anything but behind me. Suddenly the magnitude of my crisis became apparent as it only turned my ear to the sound of the giant tidal wave that was about to wash over the trajectory of our lives.

A few hours later I heard another knock on the door. Of course, at this point every knock on the door meant just another grueling twist to the plot in my real-life mystery thriller. I peeled my face off of the pillow I had been sobbing in for the past few hours and Reluctantly opened the door. Once again, there was a man whom I had never met standing behind it. He asked me to confirm my name, then handed me a small stack of papers.

"What's this?" I said as I glanced down in disbelief at what looked like legal documents. Whatever he said after that got lost somewhere in the sirens going off in my head, and the words that were printed jumped out like bullets from the page and into my sinking heart. The man at the door disappeared down the stairs as my eyes continued to navigate through the paperwork. I saw the baseline of my struggles morphed into a falsehood of my character and parenting that I could surely prove otherwise until I looked further down the page.

"Oh my God!" The room around me began to spin as my eyes fell on the photos I had taken of Lily a few weeks prior. The ones where she was wearing the sequin dress and feather boa. But they didn't look like the photos I had taken. Instead, the colored pictures had been Xeroxed using black ink, to such an extent it was difficult to see if she was even wearing anything at all! At least on her bottom half. I had assumed someone reported them as inappropriate online because of the makeup or maybe the feather boa seeming too mature for a three-year-old, even if it was just for play. I mean, I *was* in the conservative South, after all. But these? These were not the same pictures. Of course, I couldn't prove otherwise as I had deleted the original, colored photos as instructed by the scary men at my door just the day before. And by the way, I'm still not exactly sure who those men were.

Although there was something inside me that said, "Okay, someone can't just accuse you of a bunch of things that never happened, then clearly alter a picture you took and distort your intentions of it, right?" There was also something inside me that said, "Leah, you are in *that* movie. You are screwed!"

Suddenly the last several months began flashing through my mind like pieces of a jigsaw puzzle as vague clues came back to haunt me. I remembered Ryan convincing me to dance, then to move out of state. When he didn't pay child support, he gladly gave me a list of the strip clubs in the area that I could work at to support myself in this "new state." He always managed to assure me that he still cared about me and that he would always have Lily's and my best interests in mind. Even when his harsh actions contradicted his smooth words, he assured me this insensitive facade he portrayed was solely to avoid igniting his girlfriend's jealous tendencies.

I wanted to believe him! Surprisingly enough, it was difficult not to. Although the dictator-like role he took on in our marriage was oppressive, it left me believing in little else even when it was over. Deep down I was convinced I could do nothing apart from his counsel. I had spent four years conforming to someone else's decisions and direction simply because I didn't value my own competence. We had gone to war against each other, yes.

But there was also a time we shared a vulnerability with one another as well. I'd found it difficult if not impossible to convince my psyche that this person was just not safe anymore. Some of his advice I followed, obviously, and some I absolutely did not, like when he tried to talk me into switching the doorknob around to Lily's room in order to lock her in at night. It seemed even the bad advice I didn't take he still accused me of doing in the end anyway.

Just about all of Ryan's helpful guidance had a precise destination in mind, and it became clear my life and my child's life were being led strategically and connivingly toward the palm of his hand. I was so busy being hurt, feeling offended, and trying to prove myself to everyone that I was completely blind to the fatal trap I was walking right into. The paperwork went on to state that I was having my daughter appear as a child prostitute by having her pose in a sexually oriented setting. The lies were abundant, but this one was by far the most appalling.

I couldn't believe how low Ryan had stooped. I felt betrayed, I felt misunderstood, but mostly I was worried about my little girl. What were they telling her? Was she asking for me? Was she wondering why she couldn't come home? As upsetting as it was to read the outrageous allegations, I was certain that there was no way anyone would believe this craziness. Still, I began reaching out to attorneys that same Friday afternoon, but of course I was unable to find anyone to represent me that following Monday morning especially with the little money I had available for legal fees. I can only assume the timing was also part of Ryan's plan considering I was served these papers just before the weekend. Despite the odds stacking up against me, I was hopeful as my boyfriend, Mark, helped me write out my own affidavit in response to the allegations, which I confidently carried into the hearing with me the following Monday morning.

When I stepped into the courtroom, my eyes immediately landed on the woman directly in front of me casually slouched over the large wooden bench. She seemed much less studious and dignified than any judge I had ever seen on TV or had personally approached for minor traffic violations. Her demeanor resembled that of a bartender at a local dive bar more than someone in such a prominent position in the judicial system. She stared at me with empty eyes from across the room as she leaned into the podium in front of her much like a haggard bartender might lean across a counter and snarl, "What'll it be?" to his thirsty patrons.

"Where did they find this lady?" I thought. "Is she for real? Does the future of my life and the life of my child depend on *this* chick's discretion?" All I wanted to do was click my heels together and chant, "There's no place like home. There's no place like home." Then I watched a Georgia court case play out just as shadily as all other so-called legal professionals I had encountered in this strange town.

She went back and forth between myself and Ryan's attorney, but the look in her eye quickly told me who she was willing to listen to and who she wasn't. I had been a stripper in the conservative South. I had a scarlet letter across my chest that read much louder to her than any motherhood role I had been living out for the past three years. Suddenly my controversial occupation became the ripe foundation on which to build the perfect scandalous scenario.

As she began to hand over full temporary custody to Ryan based on "what he said," Mark tugged on my sleeve and whispered, "You need to tell her about the child support."

I promptly stood up and said, "Your Honor, he is over two thousand dollars behind in child support payments, according to our Illinois order."

"Welp, I don't know nothin' 'bout no Illinois order," she replied. "I ain't got nothing to do with that, but I will ask that the plaintiff pay the balance owed to the defendant." The next thing I knew, her gavel struck a deadly crack into the room. One that would reverberate into the rest of our lives. I stood there shocked for a moment as a new reality settled in. That was it. She was gone. There was no plan to restore any sort of visitation, let alone motherhood. No future hearing scheduled to investigate the serious allegations altering the trajectory of my life and the life of my child. There was no drug test, parenting class, request to bring in paperwork to prove something otherwise. It was simple. I had been a stripper, which apparently made me a blank page for anyone to write whatever they wished upon my character and call it fact. A conveniently designed arrangement to eliminate me from my child's life forever.

I walked out of that courtroom with an indescribable weight that pressed itself down into the greatest depths of my soul. A heaviness that pulled on every limb and summoned every tear to respond to its great force. My weak legs carried me as far as they could—away from the judge, away from the attorney, and away from all the people who could revel in my uncontrollable grief—as I eventually surrendered to the immense weight and collapsed to the floor. Immediately, everything inside me burst out of the tightly sealed composure I was attempting to confine it in, and the severing of my heart left me weeping relentlessly across the industrial grade carpet. I'm sure my cries could be heard down the short hallway and probably startled anyone within earshot of my resounding grief, the haunting sounds of raw, uninhibited emotion likely reaching every pocket of that building.

My body cried out just like any grieving mother's would whose child had been ripped away from her arms and who had been thrown into the death of a lie. Suddenly my little girl was on the other side of the Berlin Wall, and I could not reach her even if I tried. When she cried out for me, I wouldn't be able to console her. When she missed me, she wouldn't find me. When she needed her mommy, she would not have one. A great wave of regret swallowed me up into its powerful undertow, as a deep sadness for my baby girl surpassed any pride or desire for retaliation against anyone. In the end it was just about her. The moment was sobering and devastating all at the same time, and I lay defeated in the dust while my three-year-old daughter was whisked away on the violent winds of deceit and revenge.

Mark stood awkwardly over me in his pleated dress pants and button-up shirt, as he tried to locate the magic words to peel me off the floor.

"At least you're getting over two grand in child support money," he said in an attempt to point out the bright side of hell. I looked up at him from the floor with a grave frustration in my eyes.

"Oh my God! I don't care about the money!" I sobbed as if I was declaring it to myself, to God, and to anyone out there anywhere who would try to drive, lure, and manipulate me into believing that money could fix everything. That its power could provide freedom, confidence, and protection from heartache.

The Aftermath

I remembered how Ryan looked me straight in the eyes upon completion of our mediation agreement in Illinois over a year prior to this moment. He said to me, "You can never get rid of me because we have a child together." Although it sounded rather creepy at the time, I only assumed it meant we would always be in each other's life. I never imagined our daughter would be used as a pawn by her father to unleash his resentment toward me and maintain dictatorship over our lives for years to come. Although Ryan may have had a love for his child, it seemed his bitterness toward me was bigger than any love he had for anyone, including himself. His deceitful, hostile actions never exhibited a sincere desire for Lily's well-being; rather, it was his turn to act out on his own hurt. Although his yoke smelled less like alcohol and cut more like a knife, he had his own yoke nonetheless. Ryan's pain manifested itself in the butchering of my character and the severing of my motherhood. He had picked up his rod and struck our lives so hard I wondered if mine and my daughter's relationship would survive the destructive blow. It seemed several months of my personal struggle was enough to take several years of fierce love and commitment to my daughter and dissolve it into an entirely different substance. Disfiguring it completely.

I wondered if Lily would remember me. Remember us. The songs we would sing while taking flight on a swing set, with her small legs wrapped tightly around my hips as our stomachs cascaded into the afternoon sky. Our "picnics on the floor," as we called them, when we would gather small snacks from the kitchen, a blanket from her room, and set up a quaint little dining spot in the middle of the floor. What would happen to our neighborhood walks that we turned into magical safari adventures or our snuggles on the couch with her head in my lap as I grazed her soft round cheeks with my fingertips. All of "our things" that we did together—would they become the casualties of revenge? Would her memories of us be viciously snatched away and replaced with the false stories Ryan was convincing everyone to believe, including himself?

Could our bond stand up against his powerful words or the time and distance between us? Would she feel abandoned by me, or would she know in her heart that I longed to be near her? I wondered if she could thrive beneath the weight of her father's heavy grudge, or would her bright spirit fade inside his emotional absence or his girlfriend's toxic insecurities?

My heart flinched at the sharp edges of the despairing possibilities, while fear roared violently through each one of Ryan's ruthless intentions. The madness was so great that I only became more desperate for something greater. I found my only real refuge at the feet of Jesus. I held fast to a God who says if he begins "a good work" in us, he is faithful to "complete it" (Philippians 1:6 NKJV). I knew that my child was a gift from God to me. That our connection and my role in her life were special. Although the blades would cut us deeply, our bond would never be severed. What God has put together, no man, lie, court system, or act of revenge can ever rip apart. While the circumstances throughout the coming years would laugh in our faces and spit on our souls, God's faithfulness would never disappoint.

Even Though I'm Broken . . .

The Bible says that even while the prodigal was still far off in the distance, his father saw him and began running to him, his urgent stride fueled with compassion. When he reached his son, he fell into his arms and kissed him. The prodigal immediately began apologizing to his father, but his dad was too preoccupied with joy and relief to respond as he simultaneously began celebrating the return of his long-lost son.

> But the father said to his servants, "Quick! Bring the best robe and put it on him. Put a ring on his finger and sandals on his feet. Bring the fattened calf and kill it. Let's have a feast and celebrate. For this son of mine was dead and is alive again; he was lost and is found."
>
> (Luke 15:22–24)

Instead of allowing the hatred and shame from my accusers to define me and my relationship with my child, I

179

chose to allow God's grace to cover us. I received his forgiveness, humbly accepted the robe, and wore the ring he so lovingly slipped on my finger. Regardless of what I had done or what others were doing to me, I was a child of God. I was dead but I became alive again; I was lost but I had been found. I was wounded but I was not severed.

Chapter Ten

The Mess of Metamorphosis

In the children's book *The Very Hungry Caterpillar* written by Eric Carle, a tiny egg hatches on a leaf before a frail little caterpillar emerges from its shell. The small creature must be famished, as it immediately begins eating escalating quantities of food upon its arrival into the world. Finally, the caterpillar is so big and fat, it stops eating all together. It finds a nice safe leaf to anchor itself to as it hangs upside down and begins weaving a silk-like substance around its now-plump little body. It remains encased in this sticky haven for several days before it magically busts out of the cocoon and makes its big debut as a beautiful, majestic butterfly!

While this playful tale of metamorphosis is very charming, with its silly food options and colorful illustrations, the real-life process of a caterpillar turning into a butterfly is rather complicated and messy. Until you understand the unpleasant details of what happens inside the solitary confines of the cocoon, you can't fully appreciate the fantastic phenomenon behind this extraordinary transformation.

Let's start with the caterpillar, a creature that spends most of his life satisfying his hunger through the constant consumption of leaves. He then spins his entire body into a cocoon where he will actually digest himself until his entire being has become completely liquified! The only way for the caterpillar to become anything other than, well, a caterpillar, is to lose himself entirely. While some parts of him are transformed during this process, others will disappear from his life forever.

My Cocoon

My apartment number was 911, which couldn't have been more appropriate considering the state of emergency my life had taken since I obtained the key to this apartment home. The moment my dad and a friend from his church arrived to help me move, I was standing under a gloomy sky with my neighbor friends, blowing cigarette smoke up into the chilly afternoon air. The U-Haul truck could have very well pulled into the lot with a giant red cape swinging from its taillights along with a bold letter *S* stamped onto the hood. Except the *S* would not stand for super; instead, it would have been symbolic of second chances. It was God's grace on wheels, as it arrived without judgment, without haughty looks, only a representation of the hands and feet of Christ.

After packing up my belongings, we slowly pulled out of the very belly of my rock bottom. I waved good-bye to my friends and to the endless consumption of all the things that falsely promised to ward off spiritual hunger pangs. Everything I had stuffed myself with seemed only to leave me fat on consequences, and consequences were all I had left to take with me back to Illinois. Besides a truck full of crap that lost its value to me soon after I purchased it, I felt like I was driving away with nothing more than the breath inside my lungs.

The farther we got down the road, the more my small caravan seemed to resemble a helicopter retrieving the wounded from a battlefield, yet I was the only one fortunate enough to make the trip. As the distance grew between myself and the ones I was leaving behind, so did the compassion in my heart for those very people. Sure, I would see my neighbors soon enough since my dealings in Georgia were far from over, but it would never be under the same circumstances or with the same perspective. I was abandoning a lifestyle and a mentality that we shared in exchange for an opportunity to take control of the trajectory of my life.

I thought about the girls I worked with at the club. Did they have a place to go should they decide to regroup, to heal, to fight for their lives?

I wasn't only making my way across the county lines of Mapleview, Georgia; I was entering into a process that would completely transform me from one creature to another. Like a caterpillar makes its way from the ground to a suitable place to begin its intricate transformation into a butterfly, I was headed to my cocoon.

My hope in returning to Illinois was not only to recuperate personally but also to reestablish full custody of my child. I was committed to pursuing a deeper, more personal relationship with God as well as a healthy relationship with myself. As soon as my feet hit Illinois soil, I went to work assembling all the significant variables essential for the construction of my very own cocoon—one that would later include numerous recorded episodes of Joyce Meyer Ministries and minimal contact with old friends and bad habits. While my newly recommitted life to Christ was willing, my flesh was still rather weak. I can't say that my mentality changed right when I decided to change it. Instead, I had to surround myself with voices and environments that supported and encouraged that change.

While my parents provided a place for me to incubate spiritually, I still would have to let some physical things go. I simply did not have the means to keep up with all the financial responsibilities that maybe I could have as a stripper, nor could I assume my debt or my temptation to splurge on myself was anyone else's responsibility. I decided that getting my life together emotionally and spiritually was far more valuable to me and my daughter than any financial asset or credit score. This meant abandoning the prideful and materialistic principles that lured me into this mess in the first place. Instead, I began liquidating myself in every way. I knew that I had been drawing my value from not only men but superficial things such as clothes, labels, and, my favorite, designer handbags! I had spent so much time idolizing the people who had them that eventually these things became idols to me in themselves.

I heard once that what you behold you will eventually become. Your decisions will be determined by what you're focused on most. Whether your eyes are fixed on drugs or Jesus or, in my case, expensive handbags, your priorities and character will begin to morph around whatever you set your mind on. So through my liquidation process, I chose to let these things go, at least until I knew they did not define who I was or dictate my personal worth to myself any longer. I was literally detoxing from all the things that had any power over me and my perspective.

While avoiding previous escape methods from pain and insecurities can be a challenge, the absence of these pacifying diversions force one to come face-to-face with some unpleasant feelings. Suddenly I become keenly aware of emotions that I had been dodging for years, as the space for them to manifest enough to confront was finally available. While God's hand never failed to hold tight to mine in the utter darkness of my cocoon, the process of transformation would not be a pain-free one. Especially since I was not only pulling out the old tares from my heart, but I was resisting the growth of new ones as well. As Ryan and his girlfriend (who soon became his wife) only became more vindictive with their custodial power, I continued to grieve the loss of Lily.

Bitter or Better

I can't begin to describe the grief process that one experiences following forced separation from his or her child. Because of the time-consuming litigation process, I never really knew when I would see my daughter again, let alone have her back in my home permanently. Since Lily had usually slept in my bed with me at night ever since the divorce, her absence from this seemingly insignificant routine would prove to be the most painful. When the lights would go out and the busy sounds of life would retreat from the air, I was left to wrestle with thoughts and emotions that could run without restraint through the deadly quiet of night. The vacant pillow that was once occupied by chubby cheeks and slightly tousled strands of brown hair was now taunting my grieving soul without apology. Her soft, warm skin was painfully missing from my empty arms. Her tiny legs that once wrapped gently around mine were replaced with the synthetic fibers of the blanket I had purposely entangled myself in—a subconscious attempt, I suppose, to summon her ghost. Once sleep would eventually overtake me, the grief that lurked on the other side of its temporary oasis seemed to follow me even there.

Although my dreams would often times deliver my child back into my arms and allow me to hold her close once again, tragedy seemed to find its way into these precious moments as well. It chased us through each night as I flinched and squirmed powerlessly through each nightmare, until she was falling and I couldn't catch her! As she was being dragged away, she cried for me and I couldn't rescue her! As the terror of my dreams became too much, wakefulness would begin to nudge me back with reminders of the present.

Soon warm tears would make their way out of small creases, as my eyes remained closed, still sealed with sleep. I clung to the warm mass bundled up closely inside my fierce embrace. I imagined I was holding her with everything inside me, relieved that the nightmare was just that. It was just a bad dream. Here I had fought to save her through each toss and turn, each night terror threatening to take her from me, but there she was all along. Safe in my arms. Well, for a moment anyway. Until complete consciousness soon explained that the blanket I was intertwined with was not my child. It never was. I couldn't crawl out of bed and go find her. I couldn't just pick up the phone and locate her voice to soothe my worry and despair. Instead, I would have to adopt other ways to find her, to feel close to her somehow.

I found myself obsessing over the decorative details of her bedroom, covering her walls with giant pink polka dots that lay atop a warm taupe colored canvas of drywall. Her dollhouses were all set up and furnished, with each doll neatly dressed, poised, and ready for her delightful and sweet three-year-old imagination. Her favorite dresses hung neatly inside the closet, each awaiting her tiny form to fill it and twirl in it with her signature sass and organic charisma. There she was. All that I had left of her confined to a single room. A space I insisted remain untouched and only handled and viewed like the precious artifacts that lie undisturbed in a museum.

Some days all I could do was lie on the couch and cling to the life-giving words coming through the TV mounted on the wall in my parents' den. My broken spirit yielded to a screen occupied by preachers such as Bishop T. D. Jakes and Dr. Charles Stanley. Joyce Meyer, however, became my spiritual mama as God seriously used this woman's message to help navigate me out of one mind-set and into another. Her blunt, no-nonsense style of teaching God's Word was exactly what was needed to pull me out of my victim mentality and challenge me into a victorious life in Christ. She would say things like, "The only way to truly be happy is to get your mind off yourself and go help somebody else!" Or "You can suffer the pain of change or suffer remaining the way you are." She'd also claim, "You can be bitter or better, pitiful or powerful, but you can't be both."

So I went to work taking Joyce's biblical advice, desperate for a miraculous change in not only my circumstances but my heart as well. It was simple really. I knew if I remained in my caterpillar mind-set, I would never survive life. I was determined to learn what it meant to transform inside this cocoon, mostly because it was more painful to stay the same. I couldn't bear the weight of anger or bitterness anymore, and choosing love over hate was as plain as choosing to live or die. I chose to live! And with that I needed a completely new way of thinking. How does one think their way out of bitterness? Well, I quickly learned that my healing would be directly associated with my response to those who desired to hurt me. I took some of the most expensive items that I had acquired from dancing and gave them to Ryan's wife. Every time I would feel myself getting angry or frustrated by Ryan or his wife's behavior, I would stop myself and begin thinking of ways to bless them or somebody else.

Bless Those Who Curse You (With Chocolate, Of Course)

"Lily tells me you like caramel and chocolate," I said as I cheerfully handed Ryan's wife the shiny wrapped treat that I had picked up for her on the way to their house. Her face centered with mine, and without expression she snatched the candy from my hand as if I were simply returning it back into her possession. I then turned my attention to Lily, and we began to catch up on the things she had been up to since I had seen her last. I soon felt a warm stare looming down from above my head; I glanced up to find Lily's step-mom glaring down at me from her rooftop where she sat. Fiery darts shot with precision from her eyes as her teeth ripped through the chocolate squares and strings of caramel fell from her teeth and lips.

I couldn't help but crack up inside, as it was the first time I had seen anyone so miserable eating their favorite chocolate bar. Right then I felt God saying to me, "See,

Leah, if people are committed to hating you or misunderstanding you, they will continue to hate you or misunderstand. They will do this regardless of your efforts to establish peace or the mouthful of delicious chocolate dissolving in their mouth. Hate only blinds people to the truth and consoles one's pride, therefore justifying selfish behavior. Her attitude is her problem. Not yours. Just like your attitude is *your* responsibility. No one else's."

This truth was so freeing to me and absolutely essential to my heart transformation. It became clear to me that it was never really about them anyway. It was my love for God, myself, and my child that persuaded me to bless my enemies. Whatever I could do to keep my joy and ward off bitterness, I was willing to do it. By blessing the ones persecuting me, I was giving God back the responsibility of convicting their hearts instead of me trying to punish their egos (which never really works anyway.) As I did this, I recognized how little power they had over me, and the statement that made to my child was priceless.

> Therefore from now on we recognize no one according to the flesh; even though we have known Christ according to the flesh, yet now we know Him in this way no longer. Therefore if anyone is in Christ, he is a new creature; the old things passed away; behold, new things have come. Now all these things are from God, who reconciled us to Himself through Christ and gave us the ministry of reconciliation. (2 Corinthians 5:16–18 NASB)

The Breakout!

Once the formation of the butterfly is complete, the beautiful new creature has to work and wriggle his way out of his cocoon. The most interesting thing to me about the caterpillar's triumphant escape is that although he is now equipped with wings, without the struggle to break free, he will never fly! The strenuous fight and vigorous toil to break out of what binds him actually pushes the heavy toxins out of his still-swollen body, eliminating the weight that still confines him to a life subjected to the ground. These same toxins that were hindering his flight are then pushed into the fresh new delicate wings, inflating them into their fullest, most effective potential.

Had I not had to battle my own flesh and do right while I still felt wrong, I don't believe that I could have ever made it in the dark desolate season of the cocoon, let alone life outside of it. By pushing through the desire to give up, to feel sorry for myself, to submit to bitterness, I was pushing out all the heavy toxins in my soul that were preventing me from taking flight.

Each time you make a decision to bless or serve someone else while you're submerged in your own pain and frustration, you are simultaneously flushing the oppressive weight of bitterness out of your life, which can then be transfused into a joy that will actually empower your wings and propel you into your destiny!

The Bible states in Nehemiah 8:10, "The joy of the LORD is your strength" (NIV).

You actually can experience joy in the midst of turmoil! In fact, you are going to need it to muscle through your cocoon. Having joy doesn't necessarily mean you have uncontainable giddiness or excitement about your situation. Instead, it is a deep-down knowing that regardless of what is happening around you or to you, it is well with your soul. I like to think of it this way: God still has my best interest in mind, and I can always count on that regardless of how it looks or how it feels.

The View from Above

Now that the caterpillar has transformed into a completely new creature, everything about it has changed—the way it looks, the way it moves, the way it eats, and so on. However, through scientific tests it has been found that the memory of this exquisite creature is still intact. Although our whimsical flying friend has completely changed in every way, he still remembers his life as a caterpillar! This is such a cool example to me of the way God will completely transform the way we think, the way we live, the way we treat others, and yet he doesn't take away our memory of our prior lifestyle in sin. If he did, how could we ever relate with those who are still lost? We would flap our glorious wings in their fuzzy little faces as if to say, "Sucks to be down there, fool!"

Instead, we know even as new creations there is still an earth-crawling, dirt-muddling, gluttonous caterpillar on the inside of us all. When we see those struggling with substance abuse, promiscuity, gossiping, gambling, greed, and so on, we should see ourselves and offer the same compassion and good news of God's love that we would have wanted to receive ourselves.

The irony is that while the caterpillar's biggest priority is self-gratification as it seeks ways to satisfy its hunger, the butterfly's sole purpose in life is simply making more butterflies! It seems when the female butterfly is living her best life, or at least displaying her most glorious one, it is during this season that she is completely preoccupied with things other than herself. She spends most of her life as a butterfly ensuring the hundreds of eggs that she lays are securely fastened to the leaves her tiny offspring are going to survive on once they are born.

Could it be that we humans are actually living our best lives during the metamorphosis that God's Word performs in our hearts? It is when we finally "get ourselves off our minds," as Joyce puts it, start blessing those who hurt us, and start serving those around us, that our wings shine the brightest. This is when our spirits are light enough to soar to the greatest possible heights, as we experience life resurrected above the chaos and bitterness below. My prayer while breaking out of my own cocoon was always that God would resurrect my understanding of my circumstances so that my soul would not be so easily entangled in the grief and bitterness that longed to disable my wings. As long as I could see my problems and my adversaries from a perspective infused with faith and trust in God, then I was free.

The cocoon is not a permanent residence, yet it is a necessary stop along the way to healing and transformation. It's the pivotal place in the journey where we can let go of what is behind us and reach for what lies ahead. It's not a comfortable place or a fun place, but what it has inside is something the caterpillar life before the cocoon never does: hope. Trusting throughout this challenging season in what God's Word promises us will encourage and nurture us through the grueling, gut-wrenching, liquefying, beautiful

mess of metamorphosis.

But those who hope in the LORD will renew their

strength. They will soar on wings like

eagles; they will run and not grow weary,

they will walk and not be faint. (Isaiah 40:31

NIV, emphasis mine)

Chapter Eleven

Known

Mark never really fought back. It was as though he had nothing to defend or fight for. The thought of losing my love never caused his heart to so much as wince in defeat. He was cold with words that seemed strangely crafted of indestructible steal. When I called his phone, he didn't answer. Each text message left on delivered.

He had his heart neatly packed up with his reasons for leaving in a nonnegotiable compartment. My tear-infused pleas for him to stay only bounced off the indifference in his eyes, never penetrating the hardness of his heart.

He had been disappearing frequently, sometimes for a day and then a night or two, until eventually he just never came home at all.

To all who observed, I was quick to minimize the pain of being thrown away, as my circumstances demanded a soldier not a desperate, unwanted girl. I refused to react to rejection like I had in the past (basically sabotaging myself by numbing its unpleasant effects). So I felt it. With each unanswered call. With each pack of diapers I barely scraped together to buy. With each milestone my son reached. His first words, his obsession with trains, the adorable way his lip quivered when he got scared or upset. My heart instinctively reached for his father's response to delight together in each sweet moment. But no one was there. No one wanted to be there.

I signed my name to the right of each document that required the signatures of both mother and father as the line to the left remained as blank and unavailable as Mark had become in our lives. We were simply unknown. Unwanted.

The anger and the frustration that burned inside me rallied a straight-up gangsta girl with a "no you just didn't!" to rise to the occasion. I wanted to protest his audacity to leave me, reject me, but abandon our son? I wanted to slip on the boxing gloves and fight for me, fight for us, until I realized I was the only one in the ring fighting for anything at all. Once the anger dissolved, the only thing left to do was observe the giant hole that ached mercilessly inside my chest. I felt like a little kid who had been left on the curb somewhere for some stranger to scoop up and do with as they wished. I looked at my son and grieved that one day he would know this rejection from his own father. Would he feel the same hole, the same sensation of emptiness and abandonment?

When the White Knight Retreats

When Mark joined me in Illinois, it was about six months into my cocoon season. He swept in heroically on a white horse, full of chivalry and kindness and apparently smitten by my cause—someone wrapped tightly in the confines of her own grief and in a desperate pursuit of a godly perspective.

He said to me, "Where you go I will go, and where you stay I will stay. Your people will be my people and your God my God."

Well, sort of. Actually, that's what Ruth said to Naomi when she followed her grieving mother-in-law to her homeland to live with her there (Ruth 1:16 NIV). In a sense, Mark's commitment to me and my situation loosely resembled the kind of loyalty Ruth shared with her mother-in-law. He chose to leave his home and what he knew in order to sojourn with me through my grief, my transformation, and the fight for my daughter. He chose to connect to everything I was connected to.

I had gotten pregnant shortly before we actually married, as I'm sure I subconsciously thought that filling my womb with another child may dull the intense sting of missing the other. Mark seemed elated about marriage and having our own child together, while he simultaneously held my hand faithfully through the frustrating steps and disheartened meetings of my failing litigation process. He played with my hair for three days in the hospital after our son, Jude, was born and adored him as a precious gift he so proudly called his own. Still, it wouldn't be long until Mark's motivation to be a family man began deteriorating, as if his love and devotion had an indefinite expiration date. I watched a gentle, doting husband and father recede into frigid discontentment and flailing passions that would take him elsewhere.

Ignoring the Knee-jerk Reaction to Rejection

The immediate instinct that comes over you as the jagged blade of rejection pierces through your heart is simply to survive. Suddenly you're flooded with an intense adrenaline that commands you to seek revenge, cover, or allies to defend your grief. Oh, the temptation to submerge the fresh throbbing wound in mind-altering substances, lovers, shopping bags, or cake! Just avoiding the pathetic assumption that Mark's return to me would somehow reinstate my value as a woman, as a lover, or even as a human being was no small feat of its own!

I had to make a choice. Either I was going to forfeit everything that God was doing in my life to extinguish the immense thirst that had been provoked by yet another failed marriage, or I was going to dig my heels deeply into God's sustaining love.

I surrendered to the grief process by giving myself permission to acknowledge my injuries as a result of being vulnerable—admitting that, yes, someone still has the ability to hurt me, that I wasn't as strong or desensitized as I had desired to be or even pretended to be in the past. Only upon confessing my brokenness could I turn directly to my healer to restore me, as I plunged headfirst into the infinite companionship of Christ.

God Overcompensates

You may already know the Bible story of Leah and Rachel. Even if you do in fact know it, there's a good chance you haven't thought of it from this perspective before: Leah's perspective.

Growing up in church I often got the same response upon someone learning my name for the first time.

"Your name is Leah? Like Leah in the Bible, Leah?"

"Yup, just like that Leah." I cringed as my name (which I usually liked by the way) was once again connected to that unwanted, unattractive woman in the Bible. The ugly sister whom Jacob was tricked into marrying. The one whose groom woke up to her, after sleeping with her the night before, and was ready to trade her in for someone else immediately. I thought, "Ew, gross! Please don't associate my name with *that* Leah. I'd rather my name be affiliated with her sister Rachel. The hot one who actually had the heart of her husband, Jacob."

After being tricked into marrying Leah, Jacob had to wait a whole week before he could marry Rachel and promise to work another seven years for his father-in-law (see Genesis 29). Leah always seemed to me like the unfortunate antagonist in this romantic tale, the one who polluted a perfectly gush-worthy love story. It should have just ended with Jacob and Rachel living happily ever after without the drama of two sisters fighting over the same husband. But when I read this story after the rejection I experienced in my last marriage, a different narrative arose from the pages and penetrated the desperation in my own heart. Suddenly Leah was just as hurt, if not more, in her situation as anyone else in this story! First of all, could you even imagine your new husband anticipating the ending of your entire wedding celebration just so he could finally be with the one he *really* wanted in the first place? This was just the beginning of Leah's journey through rejection. As their days together unfolded, so did the great pain in her heart.

Upon marrying Rachel, Jacob chose to live with her instead of Leah. I wonder how insignificant Leah felt. Sure, Jacob came by her place and slept with her every now and then, but I'm pretty sure it was Rachel that he made love to and most certainly came home to every night.

The Bible says that when God saw that Leah was unloved, he opened her womb so that she may conceive children and closed the womb of Rachel so she could not. Leah went on to have three sons, each with the anticipation of finally receiving the love of her husband. The first child she named Reuben, which means "See, a son," for she said, "Because the LORD has seen my humiliation and suffering, now my husband will love me" (Genesis 29:32 AMP).

Her second son she named Simeon, which means "God hears," and she said, "Because the LORD heard that I am unloved, He has given me this son also" (Genesis 29:33 AMP).

She conceived and gave birth to a third son and said, "Now this time my husband will be attached to me, for I have borne him three sons," and she named him Levi, which means "joined" (Genesis 29:34 ESV).

This woman bore three babies in an attempt to win her husband's affections! Her plea for his love to be reciprocated was undeniable as each child's name cried out, "Love me, hear me, attach yourself to me," and yet Jacob's heart was still for Rachel alone.

It wasn't until Leah bore her fourth son that she would simply say, "Now I will praise the Lord," and she called him Judah, which means "praise" (Genesis 29:35 NKJV).

It seemed Leah had finally discovered the secret to true happiness. She decided that regardless of how her husband felt about her, she was going to praise the God who was clearly madly in love with her. Her husband may not have seen and known her, but the adoring, passionate God who created her did. He gifted her son after son after son while Rachel's womb remained closed during this time. I assume that Judah's birth was probably the most fulfilling moment in Leah's life, as her happiness and validation were finally not dependent on her husband's or anyone else's approval of her. Her heart was simply centered on God's goodness and overwhelmed by his love for her.

My Very Own Jude (Judah)

When I named my son Jude (the modern version of Judah), I had no idea that Judah in the Bible was the son of Leah, let alone what it meant and why she named him that. By the time I gave birth to my own son Jude, I was completely enveloped in my own thankfulness to God. I knew that it was a miracle that I was even still alive, let alone cradling a beautiful baby boy of my own. When I looked into Jude's eyes, I saw the unfailing, relentless love of God. I couldn't help but believe, like Leah did, that he saw my affliction and had blessed me with my very own Jude, my reason to praise.

Jude's sweet cuddles and soft, warm skin would console me every time my heart was pierced with loneliness or discouragement. His presence was soothing and always reminded me of God's faithfulness and affections in the midst of sorrow and disappointment. Jude's life was a testament to me of the tangible way God redeems our lives regardless of whether we think we deserve it or not. His love for us is nonnegotiable, indestructible, and completely independent of anyone else's opinion of us.

Yada

After Mark left, I stayed abstinent because, well, it was the right thing to do. I mean, the Bible does say not to have sex outside the confines of marriage, so I wanted to honor that because I simply wanted to honor God. Shortly after Mark's disappearance, I attended a women's conference at a church I had visited quite a few times in Georgia during my ongoing custodial battle there. The conference was called Apple of His Eye and held maybe three or four services over the course of the weekend. The services included several guest speakers as well as incredible praise and worship experiences. One particular service I attended, however, was especially life changing for me. I remember being amused yet inspired as I watched this beautiful blonde woman boldly take the stage and deliver her powerful message with a thick Southern drawl and a feisty Holy Ghost sass.

She began to break down a verse in the Bible where God tells Jeremiah that he "knew" him before he had even formed him in his mother's womb (Jeremiah 1:5). The interesting thing about this verse is that the word "knew" is also used in the book of Genesis when Adam lay with, or "knew," his wife, Eve. The word *knew* actually comes from the word *yada* in Hebrew, and *yada* means "intimacy," also "to know," "to be known," and "to be perceived."[1] Jeremiah had known an intimacy with God before he ever knew life here on earth. God had already known him thoroughly and loved him unconditionally before he was even born! This got me thinking.

Could it be that our deep longing for intimacy (to be known) was ignited from a time we won't ever remember? Like before we were even born? Do we venture through our lives longing, seeking, and yearning for something we have already experienced? It's almost like we sense its absence, as if something is missing that we know should be there. We look for it in our relationships, our spouses, lovers, pornography, social media, but nothing quite satisfies us.

---

[1]. "Yada," BibleStudyTools.com, accessed November 15, 2019, https://www.biblestudytools.com/lexicons/hebrew/kjv/yada.html.

At least not for long. We may have moments that resemble yada, or even imitate it, but when is it the real thing?

What if I told you that God gives us the perfect example of what real intimacy looks like through the manifestation of his presence here on this earth. If you've ever been in the tangible presence of God, you would probably agree that it is the most amazing feeling one can ever encounter. It's this supernatural sensation of being completely swallowed up by something not only bigger than you but bigger than anything you've ever known or ever will know. It's as if your soul is being temporarily elevated from the weight of this earth, until everything that was triggering you before becomes either irrelevant or trivial. As you become wrapped up securely in the perfect love of God, a love that casts out *all* fear, you find yourself completely known yet still completely adored and delighted in. You are safe! You are pure! You are completely free! If

I had to describe it with only one word, I would simply say it is beautiful.

Relationships with conditions are what we know, what we're used to. Our value to others is simply dependent on the fickle chemicals going off in our brains at any given time. We are flawed, disposable, and common in this world. But when God looks at us, he examines us with sweet endearment. He knows our thoughts, the number of hairs on our heads. We are special! We are precious! We are the "apple of his eye."

And there it was. As if a bolt of lightning lit up the room and struck my soul directly. For the first time ever, I had a clear revelation of my own spiritual thirst. All of these years I had been suppressing it, condemning it, exploiting it, smoking it, drinking it, sleeping with it, and so on. I had been so ashamed of it, as I assumed it was just an unfortunate, instinctual thorn given to each of us through the fall of man. One we would fight and wrestle with in the depths of our unsuccessful prayers and persistent repentance only to fall prey to its beckoning once more. Who knew it was actually intentionally placed on the inside of us, to point us back to the real source who developed it in the first place.

I was dumbfounded at how deceived I had been in my own attempts to satisfy it. How I had relied on a defective and deficient culture to define what intimacy was for me instead of realizing the beautiful gift God had designed it to be. The powerful connection of two souls during sex is in fact a spiritual bond you make with another. It's a surrender to each other's hearts. It's a sanctuary created *by* God for you to be known and to fully know the one whom you've made a lasting covenant with. It's a place to be vulnerable, safe, and completely free! It's a refuge to disarm in. To heal in. An attempt to better grasp the beautiful intense love that God has created us in. I mean, sex was in fact designed by God, regardless of how some holy rollers may demonize it or how this world may deform and pervert it.

Not only could I finally comprehend what God desires for us to experience as human beings with each other; I also had an incredible revelation of God's intimate, passionate love for me! I belonged to him! I was his bride! I was spoken for by the God of the universe! Suddenly the rejection that came with the abandonment of my son's father, or with any other relationship, lost power over my worth and self-confidence. I felt God's Word cover me as I now had a direct reference of what real love looks like, what intimacy really was, and what it meant to be pursued by real love.

Finally I had a real reason to honor my body. I wasn't as comfortable wearing some of the clothes I used to wear in the past—the ones that assured me I was only attractive or even visible if something was hanging out. I had a conviction about giving myself away sexually because in a sense I was already taken. I became more cautious of situations and of men I felt may expect me to compromise my convictions or didn't share them with me. I wasn't perfect by any means, but I strove to honor the beautiful communion I had with God. The Bible says, "Above all else, guard your heart, for everything you do flows from it" (Proverbs 4:23 NIV).

I was tired of the same toxic issues in my life, so guarding my heart was a must. I was protecting something God told me to protect because I was actually valuable to him. My new limitations never felt confining but instead were liberating. I felt safe and special in the boundaries of true love.

Remembering Your Source

Although sex inside the covenant of marriage should resemble the incredible intimacy God designed for it, unfortunately that doesn't mean that it automatically does. God commands husbands to love their wives and wives to submit to their husbands for a reason. Only upon following God's perfect recipe for creating a safe space for intimacy to grow will we actually be able to experience it with each other.

Maybe some of you are still waiting to meet your person, or marry your person. Maybe you *have* met him, you *have* married him, but this kind of intimacy is completely absent in your relationship. It's one thing to be hopeful as you wait for love, but what if you waited yet what you waited for is not at all what you hoped for? Would if it's lacking the very thing you were counting on, intimacy?

Your spouse may take out the trash, pay the bills, or even be the best father you could ever imagine to your children, yet there's something significant missing. It's a substance and connection in which a union must be anchored in order to survive. It's a key component that cannot be ignored. At least not forever, as eventually resentment begins to weaken the foundation as priorities and hearts get tucked away in forgotten compartments that eventually become unavailable, even unrecognizable.

Jesus said in Matthew 19:8 that Moses had permitted divorce because of the husbands' hard hearts for their wives, but that was not what God had originally intended for us. Yet isn't this how it begins, one heart growing hard, or cold, toward the other?

He might not be walking out the door physically, but he walks out on you emotionally every single day. When you reach for him, he turns away. When you look deep into his eyes, you cannot find him. Maybe he touches you but he doesn't see you.

It's easy to believe that it's sex or romance that we're longing for or missing in the relationship, but it's actually so much more. We all want to be seen, heard, loved. We all want to be "known."

What happens when the one you love, the one you've given yourself to, your virginity, your time, your life, doesn't want to "know" you anymore? Has your value expired, or is your spouse struggling to surrender to what God has called him to do in the relationship? It's too easy to take someone else's struggle personally and immediately want to defend ourselves, victimize ourselves, or try to "fix" ourselves to reach an impossible expectation that, let's be honest, at the end of the day has nothing to do with us.

Their struggle to do what God has called them to do cannot define us, nor can it dictate our own behavior. It cannot measure our worth, and it certainly does not interfere with our value in Christ! This doesn't mean that we don't take responsibility for our own shortcomings or struggles in the relationship, but it gives us a clearer perspective of what *our* role is in the marriage, and believe it or not, ladies, it's not to convince him to love you. As a hairstylist, I've seen girls go from brunette to blonde to bald for love (myself included)! Unfortunately, you cannot be pretty enough, smart enough, thick, thin, or thrifty enough, to be pursued, celebrated, or loved by your husband. All real love and intimacy come from God, and we cannot force it to flow through the people that we assume it should. But be assured and take comfort in the fact that God sees your broken heart—just as he saw Leah's.

"He will cover you with his feathers. He will shelter

you with his wings. His faithful promises are

your armor and protection." (Psalm 91:4

NLT)

The incredible intimacy God gifts our relationships with here on this earth is certainly amazing, yet I believe he allows us to experience the disappointment that we do with people so that we won't forget the source from which it comes. Otherwise, it's too easy for us to idolize others instead of worshiping the God who created them.

After I had married my third husband, JD, I couldn't wait to experience this yada, or intimacy, in my new, God-centered marriage. Although we both anticipated this incredible connection, when it wasn't immediate, we both became impatient and discouraged. I mean, we had only known each other for a few months, so needless to say, it just wasn't there yet. Over time, we only became more disappointed with each other and definitely let the other know it! (Perfect way to build intimacy by the way.)

I felt incredibly confused and frustrated, considering the fact that I was positive God told me I would have this beautiful connection with my husband. I was like, "Um . . . God? Did I click on the wrong dude on eHarmony? Because this fella has nooooo interest in loving me like that." In fact, I was pretty sure he hated my guts half the time. I would cry for love, I would beg for love, kick, stomp, and pout for love! Yet all I got was a stone-cold stare that slammed every door to his heart on the desperation of mine. He always had an excuse for his rejection, but when all the excuses were resolved, his love was *still* unavailable.

Finally I looked at God and said, "Why would you show me this amazing revelation of real intimacy and how beautiful and wonderful it is, then have me marry this guy who is literally a brick wall? Why would you tease me like that?" Then God began to show me that through my frustration with my husband's rejection, I had forgotten my true source. I had become insecure, lonely, bitter, and resentful trying to drink love from an empty cup. Then I heard God say, "Let *me* tell you how beautiful you are. Let *me* sweep you off your feet. I will never stop pursuing your heart even when he does."

God reminded me that although I wasn't single anymore, he still needed to be my number one source of intimacy. And friends, let me tell you, God is chivalrous! He will show up in the little things. The big things. The simple things. He will comfort you through the perfect song serenading you through your car stereo system, holding you in its lyrical embrace as you release to him the weight of your crumbling day. He will lavish you with the warmth of his smile through the sunlight that cascades across your brow and playfully dances over the delicate strokes of your eyelashes. His gentleness peeks through the leaves that sway delicately outside your bedroom window. His voice can be heard in the bouquet of his creation as sweet colorful birds sing harmoniously for your pleasure. His affections will comb through the tresses of your hair as a breeze sweeps across your gaze and into the masterpiece he's painted for you in the evening sky.

He's protective of you as "he will command his angels concerning you to guard you in all your ways . . . so that you will not strike your foot against a stone" (Psalm 91:11–12 NIV).

He's in the hug from that person who saw you and just knew you needed one. He knows you love ice cream, so that coupon for a complimentary ice cream cone you got in the mail was *all* him!

When I began to take my need to be known off my husband and put it back on God, he once again swallowed me up in his limitless love and companionship. My thoughts were no longer consumed with who *wasn't* loving me; instead, they were preoccupied by who *is*! Soon I began to see God work in my husband's heart as well, as only he could. He began to show me that although I wasn't seeing his promises unfold for my marriage as soon as we said "I do," that did not mean that I never would. Instead, I had to trust the God who revealed such promises to me in the first place, to bring them to pass as well.

In the meantime, I would continue to draw from my main source of intimacy. One far beyond what we are even capable of providing for each other as human beings. I mean, how much more intimate can you get than resting in the hands that created you, the breath that breathed life into you, and the heart that is consumed by you? Someone with such a powerful passion for you that he sent his only son to this earth to die so that he could spend eternity with you! *This* is romance. *This* is love. And *this*, my friends, is what intimacy with Christ is all about. You are heard! You are seen! You are completely known and still infinitely loved.

Chapter Twelve

Shameless

Shame is a prison with bars much thicker than iron or steel. It holds one captive with just a word, a condescending look. It will convince a well-abled soul that she cannot stand, that she cannot walk. Surely she will never run. Instead, she will remain under the oppressive words spoken over her. She will be held captive by the voices that make their way into her heart and mind. There are no visible chains. No alarms to trigger. No weapons that threaten to harm her should she try to escape. Instead it's a prison that follows her wherever she goes. There is no escape! Not physically anyway. Only through the courage to believe a truth that exists beyond the darkened walls of the prison cell constructed in one's own mind.

The fatal weight of shame is designed to crush its victim into submission. Into deficiency. Even into death. It holds no physical weapon, yet it coaxes its prey into drinking the poison, pulling the trigger, or shedding the blood that is rarely found on the hands of its perpetrators. The evidence is hidden only in the broken pieces of each casualty's heart.

Shame versus Conviction

While shame and conviction might be sisters, they are certainly not twins! Although they have similar features, one is used more like a compass to keep us on the right path, while the other can get us so far off the path we wonder if we will ever find our way home at all.

Conviction is also comparable to the pain receptors we have in our bodies. You touch a hot stove, you leap back in pain. It startles you, and you immediately decide that feeling was not a good one and you don't want to experience it again. So note to self: "Avoid touching hot stove." But what happens when the very indicator that alerts you when something is wrong is the very thing that causes you to continue to hurt yourself? It's almost like touching the hot stove, flinching back, but feeling so guilty about touching it in the first place, you continue to touch it again and again as self-punishment.

Or what if you've refrained from reaching back into the penetrating heat, yet you hold yourself to the moment in which you did? You're chained to the regret and summoned by the scars to identify yourself with the disfigured aftermath of your mistakes. This is the very nature of shame.

Now, imagine if someone told you immediately after you burned yourself that you should continue to burn yourself. That it's just who you are and what you do, and it will *always* be just who you are and what you do. They might say something like, "Go ahead! Stick your hand on that hot iron griddle. You deserve the consequences!" Would you follow their instructions? Of course not! Why, then, would you let someone convince you to inflict emotional, mental pain and suffering on yourself? But this is exactly how shame works. When someone is trying to shame us, they are actually insisting that we adopt the critical opinion they have of us as our new and final self-identity. Because of this appointed identity, they believe we must live in a perpetual cycle of pain and shame. When we begin to look to others to gauge our morality and the sanctification of it, we are basically giving people permission to incarcerate our character and sentence us to a life of defeat and despair. We are completely ignoring what God says about us and the price he paid for our sins by allowing the toxic words of our haters dictate our worth and the God-given destiny he has for our lives.

While all of us are guilty of falling short and doing things that do not please God, some of us are under the impression that our crap stinks less than the next person's does—when in reality it all smells like crap to God. If God, who is the ultimate judge, isn't holding us captive to our sin and failures, then why are we allowing other sinners to hold us captive to our mistakes? More importantly, why are we holding *ourselves* hostage to their opinions and to the misconstrued conceptions we have about ourselves?

Think about the way we talk to ourselves. I don't know about you, but I could spend the entire day kicking myself for one thing or another. Then of course I wonder why I feel so small by the time I crawl into bed at night.

One evening I prayed, "Oh God, please help me! Why do I feel so dang inadequate some days? Some days I feel like I just suck at everything!" Then I heard God say, "Welp, look at how you talk to yourself all day long." He said, "Leah, you are going to be spending a lot of time with yourself. In fact, you can't get away from yourself! *You* are with *you* wherever *you* go. You might as well start liking yourself and talking to yourself the way you would like others to talk to you!"

I was like, "Oh" (slight head tilt). Well, that makes sense, right? But the thing is, I believe we have been conditioned in our culture and even through our broken relationships that being critical with ourselves, even shaming ourselves, is necessary to keep us in line or maybe even acceptable in society. That's why shaming people into Christianity, conformity, or success never works since its debilitating methods only lead to failure and disgrace. And yet, not only do we try this tactic with others when discussing our views and opinions, we subconsciously do it to ourselves all the time. I mean, how often do we compare ourselves to others in their social media feeds as we scroll through the highlights and photoshopped versions of other people's lives? No wonder so many of us are riddled with anxiety! We throw ourselves on the hot stove daily, not realizing the burns we are inflicting on our own self-confidence and the potential God has for us. We simply don't believe we are worthy.

We are chained to our guilt. Controlled by our inadequacies and paralyzed by our own insufficiencies. We recede back into our cages, declining our freedom, as we peer through the bars that isolate us from the truth.

As far as the east is from the west, so far has he

removed our transgressions from us. (Psalm

103:12 NIV)

Swimming Toward the Shark

I recently read a book called *Unwanted* written by Jay Stringer. In a chapter titled "Transforming Self," he tells a story about one of the cameramen for the Discovery Channel show *Shark Week*. The man was asked what he was supposed to do when a great white shark is swimming right at him. He said he must do something counterintuitive: "Swim directly at the shark with the camera." Since the shark is used to all the other sea creatures swimming away from it, this action seems to trigger a defense mechanism in the shark. "The reality is, if you don't act like prey, they won't treat you like prey."[2]

As Stringer explains, "Shame's power is so often derived from our flight from it. The more we run, the more it pursues us."[3]

I decided to move back down to Mapleview, Georgia shortly after my son's first birthday. Mark had completely disappeared from our lives at this point. Although the court hearings and litigation fees related to the custody battle for my daughter had subsided for a time, I knew that the rumors and backlash from my former lifestyle had not. I was climbing back into the mouth of the lion, facing the legalistic death stare that loomed over the otherwise charming community. I was stepping back into the storm that once ravaged me. The circumstances that triggered all the tares on the inside of me. I was literally

[2]. Jay Stringer, Unwanted: *How Sexual Brokenness Reveals Our Way to Healing* (Colorado Springs, CO: NavPress, 2018), page#?
[3]. Jay Stringer, *Unwanted, page# 144,145*

swimming directly at the shark with determination in my bones and the word of God in my mouth. I refused to become prey to shame once more.

Now the only difference between my first move to Mapleview and the second was simply that the stakes were much higher the second time around. The shame was thicker, money was tighter, and heck, I had *two* kids now with *two* "baby daddies—and not *one* wedding ring on my finger (judgmental people love that look by the way).

Although Ryan had primary custody of Lily, I still had her three to four days a week as long as I was residing in the same county. I was so excited to be reunited with my daughter on a regular basis that I would have moved into the depths of hell to be near her, and some days hell is where it felt like I was.

With most of my family and support system several hundreds of miles away, Mapleview almost felt like another planet that God was calling me to. I set out into this other world with just a passion for my child and God's calling on my life. I was completely surrounded by my past mistakes, living in the heart of my ground zero, alongside the people who hated me most. It was the perfect opportunity for God to receive all the glory! I soon began to see this as my mission field. I've always liked a challenge, and to me this was exactly what I was about to suit up for. My theme verse?

For we do not wrestle against flesh and blood, but

against principalities, against powers,

against the rulers of the darkness of this age.

(Ephesians 6:12 NKJV)

I had to remind myself constantly that it wasn't a certain group of people I was conflicting with; it was much deeper than that. I came into this town knowing full well there would be a spiritual battle in front of me, as this was the place that almost devoured me whole. Elated that I had survived it but angry at how close the enemy had gotten, I was walking into this new chapter ready to live and love my life and to kick shame's teeth in while doing it! Besides, I wasn't going in it alone this time. *This* time, I was believing God for everything, and leaning on my own understanding was absolutely off the table. Come hell or high water, I was going to do things *his* way.

Because the Sovereign LORD helps me, I will not be

disgraced. Therefore, I have set my face like

a stone, determined to do his will. And I

know I will not be put to shame. (Isaiah 50:7

NLT)

The Single Mom Salute

Being a single mom is no joke! And for someone as lacking in management skills as I was (and still am most of the time), this move made for a huge undertaking. The girl who was once convinced she had no other choice than to be dependent on a man to overcompensate for her inadequacies was actually forced to face them and learn how to be competent *in them*. The same girl convinced she had to use her sexuality to manipulate her circumstances and financial security was now completely dependent on her mind and her faith in God to work out her circumstances and work out her security.

It was Transformation 101, folks! But some of the most empowering moments of my life happened in this season. I couldn't completely dissolve the chains of shame that were bound to me until I was forced to prove to myself they didn't belong there. God knew exactly what I needed to learn about myself in order to unlock the prison of shame I had put myself in.

Pitiful or Powerful

Taking my crazy, hyper kids to the grocery store was a bit of a challenge of its own, but taking them to the grocery store and denying their many food requests could be deflating. Living on our tiny income was kind of like practicing intricate story problems *all the time* with every basic need. I would roam aimlessly through the local Walmart, pushing the kids in an empty shopping cart and browsing each aisle trying to find the most efficient way to stretch the little bit of money that we *did* have. I would be like, "Let's see, how do I buy gas, dinner, and a pack of diapers with this ten-dollar bill that I just got from selling some of my clothes to a nearby consignment store?"

There were times when my mind wanted to sink into how unfair things were, watching other people filling their carts with whatever their children desired while I couldn't even afford the Walmart brand diapers. Still, I never even considered going back to dancing or calling some past dude to help a girl out. Instead, when I got desperate for diapers, I made them out of paper towels and plastic Walmart bags. We ate *a lot* of oatmeal and peanut butter, and I *was* that "four dollars on pump three, please" person at the gas station.

If I had to do something like fix the vacuum or move heavy furniture, I literally prayed to God to help me with even the practical, almost humorous tasks. For the first time in my life, I saw what I was capable of doing without resorting to compromising my convictions or the path God was calling me to walk. I was so broke and so lonely at times but also so liberated and hopeful as I just simply trusted in him.

One evening when I had taken my kids for a stroll downtown, I remember Lily hanging monkey-style on my left side as I used my right arm to carry my son's stroller, with him in it, up the countless stairs that cascade throughout the beautiful park area in Downtown Mapleview; meanwhile, both kids whined and whimpered in exhaustion. I lifted and grunted in my attempt to reach the top of the steps, until I happened to look around and noticed complete families gallivanting up these endless stairs together. One parent was carrying a stroller, while another parent was giving a giggling curly-haired child a piggyback ride.

Immediately my heart ached in defeat, as the weight of abandonment and rejection began to fill up like a giant rain cloud over my spirit. Just as I began to pout, I heard God say, "Leah, you will get more from this time with me than any man could ever give you, and any devil could ever take away from you, but only if you refuse to feel sorry for yourself. You can choose to be either empowered by your circumstances or pitiful because of them."

Those words completely sobered the entire pity party going on in my head and eventually became the words I would anchor every future pity moment to. I chose to allow this season to grow something inside me that otherwise never would. For the first time in a long time, I was proud of myself! I felt strong, I felt productive, I felt alive! I went to bed every night knowing I did the best with what I had, without compromising my values to attain what I didn't.

Shame couldn't catch up with me as long as I was busy making my heavenly Father proud. I wanted to show him that I would be the best mom I could possibly be. I wanted him to know how honored I was that he had blessed me with both a boy and a girl and precious relationships with both of them. Both God and I knew how hard I worked and how much I poured into my kids and honestly, that was enough for me.

Looking For the Justice in Shame

As gossip about me gained momentum through the whispers and haughty glances that circled me in the school cafeterias, parent teacher conferences, or any other opportunity Ryan and his wife had to get into someone's head concerning me. I couldn't help but wonder when justice would finally make its grand entrance on these people who were dedicated to demonizing me as a mother, a woman, and as a human being, really. I mean, it was difficult enough to forgive myself for the things I *did* do, but to bear the shame of the things I didn't? Well, I couldn't help but look at God and say, "Okay, God! This has been going on for quite some time now. I mean, these people are *still* deeply committed to butchering me with their shame knives. Where are you in this anyway?"

Right then I began to remember how much more tangible God's presence became to me when I felt bullied or defenseless in these moments. When I was surrounded, I could always find every piece to the spiritual armor that he made readily available for me to put on. To cover myself with. To fight back with. Each piece representing something absolutely necessary to fight a battle that was not against people but, rather, against the darkness of this world: a belt of truth, a breastplate of righteousness, shoes of peace, a shield of faith, the helmet of salvation, and the sword of the spirit, which is God's Word. (Ephesians 6:14–17)

I could wrap myself up in his warm, secure embrace as I sensed him taking every fiery arrow that came at my heart and quenching it with his passionate love for me. The same shame and affliction Jesus endured on the cross for me way back then was and is the same shame and affliction he endured for me and *still* does in the presence of my haters.

Therefore the LORD longs to be gracious to you, and

therefore He waits on high to have

compassion on you. For the LORD is a God

of justice; How blessed are all those that

long for Him. (Isaiah 30:18 NASB,

emphasis mine)

I eventually learned that my justice concerning shame would not look like I thought it would nor how I had hoped it would. It didn't make its grand entrance through a court hearing, an apology, or even a change of heart. Instead, my justice would be revealed in who *I* could be regardless of how unjustly I was being treated.

When I could still be that silly, bubbly (way too excited for a school lunch visit) kind of mom in a room of people who didn't think I deserved to be there. When I could still believe that I was valuable, precious, and worthy of love as a child of God. When my joy was nonnegotiable and my heart too compassionate to be hardened. When I could spend *my* life refusing to beg for approval or kindness from theirs. *That* is when justice showed up and shame was defeated! It happened in moments that turned into days that turned into years, until it made its own sound that spoke louder than any rumor or debilitating word hanging from anyone's bitter lips. Shame had lost its power over me, and God's love was able to continue to pour through my life and into the lives of others.

Therefore we also, since we are surrounded by so great a cloud of witnesses, let us lay aside every weight, and the sin that so easily ensnares us, and let us run with endurance the race that is set before us, looking unto Jesus, the author and finisher of our faith, who for the joy that was set before Him endured the cross, despising the shame, and has sat down at the right hand of the throne of God. For consider Him who endured such hostility from sinners against Himself, lest you become weary and discouraged in your souls. (Hebrews 12:1–3 NKJV, emphasis mine)

Conclusion

Black Sheep Revival

After spending just about a year working on this book, I came to the final chapter and paused. Although my outline had already been written months ago, for the first time since I started writing this, I felt a shift in direction.

Of course, each one of the tares that I identify in each chapter I continue to surrender to God on a daily basis. There is continuous healing and growth with each day that passes and even each transparent word I have wrestled to these pages that tell my story. I've managed to congregate several moments that have created me, disassembled me, and put me back together again. I've retreated back to spaces and emotions to collect all the intricate details, both painful and wonderful, to better explain the unraveling of my issues, the recovery thereafter, and ultimately the unveiling of God's glory in my life.

In the end, though, I felt like something was missing in the completion of the story of my personal healing. A significant piece to the puzzle that I have had hidden behind my back, simply because I've never known exactly what to do with it. It has just become a normalcy to carry it around with me since unfortunately it has become a part of my life as I know it. I've attempted to associate it with the oppression of shame, and although the two can relate, they are simply different entities altogether.

In an attempt to find out what else God wanted me to say in this book, I confessed to him, "Okay, God, what am I still struggling with? What is it you still desire to heal in me?" I had an idea of what it might be, but asking God this question only illuminated the vast space this pestilent weed still occupied in my mind (or behind my back).

I shared with you the story of my father being shot and the fear of being physically inflicted myself that haunted me and my psyche for years. But what I couldn't fit into the pages of this book were the numerous gun shots that have gone off, metaphorically, throughout the past thirteen years, and continue to do so, concerning my relationship with my daughter. Although most of the bullets fired have only posed a threat to me and my child, others have not and shot indefinite holes into mine and my daughter's lives. Holes that cost us days, weeks, or even months of contact. Holes that were inflicted to teach us a lesson should we imagine freedom or confront injustice. Holes that stated, "You do what I tell you to do or else!"

Ryan said it best when we were discussing our legal situation several years ago and he disclosed to me, "Leah, it's not what you know, it's *who* you know."

After spending thousands of dollars on litigation fees and hiring four different attorneys I was still unable to regain custody of Lily. The shame that comes with living under someone else's lies or bitterness toward you is one thing, but to live beneath the fear and oppression of their control over the life you get to spend or not spend with your child is another. If I tried to stand up for me or for her, we could have lost each other forever! There was no system or child advocacy process to ensure such injustice did not occur; in fact, it occurred all the time. I found out the hard way how easily one can fall victim to a broken system when it all seems to depend on where you are, who you are, and who you know.

If I didn't speak to my ex-husband in a humble and lowly manner, he felt I was too confident in my position as "mom" and would simply make it difficult to contact my child at all.

After years of being trained to stay on a tight leash, a dog will simply be too timid to leave his master's side. Especially if the dog is struck each time it tries to resist the restraint. This seemed to become my position in my parental role with my daughter. I had become obedient and had submitted to Ryan's tyranny and bitterness for so many years that it simply became the heavy yoke that I abided by.

As our lives were yanked and pulled by each harsh command of our master, my daughter would grow frustrated by my submission to its authority. Yet, after she had seen for herself the consequences of confrontation, she then understood the confines of my position and his disregard for hers.

The same fear that had me looking under beds and behind shower curtains for a dangerous intruder when I was younger, became the same fear that would follow me around the town of Mapleview, Georgia. It stood suspiciously behind the desk of each school office, where the employees there had already read the disqualifying court documents from years past (Ryan and his wife made sure of that). It eagerly waited on each new face I met in the community, each job I applied for, and each church member I sat next to in the pews on Sunday morning.

Although I *knew* I was undeserving of the conclusions that these individuals may have come to after the endless discrediting words spoken or written about me, they still managed to detain me. Their voices united were bigger and roared more loudly than mine, so I had learned to whisper, to come under, to assume ownership of Ryan's yoke as it was placed on me.

After all the miraculous things that God had done in my life and continues to do, I have still found myself looking over my shoulder, often shrinking inside the shadows that threaten to swallow up my perceived security. As the fear of being shot at once again by my enemies dismantled my spirit, I continued to run from the penetrating sound of a threat.

When I went to God about this, I asked him, "Why am I still so traumatized by these people? Why do I feel like I have to run from them? Hide from them? Where is this boldness and trust I should have in you?" God simply answered my questions with a question: "What are you hiding?"

If I Were Gideon

Gideon was in the winepress, which was a giant hollowed-out rock in a low-lying area designed for crushing grapes for wine. He was threshing wheat there instead of on the threshing floor, which is usually situated high on a hill. Now, threshing wheat in a winepress would kind of suck considering one needs the assistance of the wind to blow away the useless, messy chaff, leaving only behind the precious grain—hence the benefits of the high hill and wind.

But Gideon was hiding the grain and for good reason. The Midianites (Israel's archenemies) had been ravaging their crops and stealing all their livestock for the past seven years!

When an angel of the LORD appeared to Gideon, he

said, *"The LORD is with you, mighty*

warrior."

"Pardon me, my Lord," Gideon replied, "but if the

LORD is with us, why has all this happened

to us? *Where are all his wonders that our*

ancestors told us about when they said, 'Did

not the LORD bring us out of Egypt?' But

now the LORD has abandoned us and given

us into the hand of Midian."

The LORD turned to him and said, "Go in the

strength you have and save Israel out of

Midian's hand. Am I not sending you?"

"Pardon me, my lord, "Gideon replied, "but how

can I save Israel? My clan is the weakest in

Manasseh, and I am the least in my family."

The LORD answered," I will be with you, and you

will strike down all the Midianites, leaving

none alive." (Judges 6:12–16 NIV, emphasis

mine)

Now, *my* conversation with God would go
something like this:

"Um . . . pardon me, God, but these people are
bullies! They manage to convince others to be bullies,
which ultimately leads to me either not seeing my child or
being treated like absolute garbage!" And the Lord replied,
"Am I not sending you?"

Maybe I haven't been sent by God to take out the
Ryaninites with a physical sword, but I am called to draw
my spiritual one. By applying the Word of God to my
adversaries' tactics, I can combat evil with good, hate with
love, and shame with glory!

How many people fight some sort of Midianite in
their lives every single day? Maybe yours is a familite, ex-
husbandite, jobite, bossite, or cellulite! Whatever your "ite"
is, has it caused you to hide as mine has? Has it convinced

you to carry a yoke that discredits you, isolates you, or torments you with fear?

The more I thought about this, the more evident the real root to my issue had become, and I asked myself, "Have I hidden my testimony in the winepress or behind my back because I was afraid of what my enemies might do with it? Afraid they would pervert it somehow or use it as another platform to slander me as they had done in the past?"

Regardless, God has called me to take his good works to the threshing floor—high on a hill where it can be seen and heard and reach the hearts of others while glorifying God!

My dialogue with God continued:

"Pardon me, Lord, but I am the black sheep of the family. I am not super successful by the world's standards. Besides, how can I do anything with these 'ites' and their persistent shaming and threatening?" And God replied,

"Leah, you wouldn't have this testimony if you didn't have enemies. Does this small group of people represent the whole world? Do those people represent the ones you know are hurting in similar ways that you have? Have I called you to write this for your enemies or in spite of them? Their criticism and shame is their prison, but it does not have to be yours. As long as you listen and believe what I say about you and not what they say about you, you will be free. You will be bold. You will be everything I'm calling you to be."

Revival: Restoration to Life, Consciousness, Vigor, Strength

If my testimony could help deliver someone else out of the hand of fear, rejection, shame, addiction, or insecurity, then I am willing to leave the winepress and thresh my testimony on a high hill for the Holy Spirit to do with it whatever he pleases.

God has preserved my family, my sanity, and ultimately my life so that I could be used by him to breathe life into others. My prayer as I end this final chapter is that you will have seen the rich, tangible love of God through a book filled with one girl's story of life, loss, and redemption through Christ.

I want to encourage people with friends or family who are running full speed in the wrong direction.

Above all, love each other deeply, because love

covers over a multitude of sins. (1 Peter 4:8

NIV)

I want to encourage the person who's reading this and may feel stuck in any one of the tares I've described. There is a way out! Refuse to believe otherwise! Take God's hand and allow him in to where you are, wherever that may be. He longs to be with you, to heal you, to restore you!

Revival begins at surrender, and surrender begins with each one of us. Whether we are the black sheep, the blue sheep, whatever color sheep, we are *all* desperate for the love and grace of our heavenly Father.

Who will separate us from the love of Christ? Will tribulation, or distress, or persecution, or famine, or nakedness, or peril, or sword? Just as it is written,

"FOR YOUR SAKE WE ARE BEING PUT TO DEATH ALL DAY LONG; WE WERE CONSIDERED AS SHEEP TO BE SLAUGHTERED."

But in all these things we overwhelmingly conquer through Him who loved us. For I am convinced that neither death, nor life, nor angels, nor principalities, nor things present, nor things to come, nor powers, nor height, nor depth, nor any other created thing, will be able to separate us from the love of God, which is in Christ Jesus our Lord. (Romans

8:35–39 NASB)

ACKNOWLEDGMENTS

To my parents ~ You have been the hands and feet of Jesus to me and my children. I'm certain I would not be here today had you not so selflessly represented the great love and compassion of Christ. You have walked through so many of these moments of crisis with me and many more that these pages simply cannot hold. I am forever grateful for your unwavering love and support!

To my husband JD ~ You have heard more about this book than I'm sure anyone would ever care to! The way you have encouraged me to pursue something that God has put on my heart to do has been nothing less than fortifying and inspiring. I'm so blessed to have you beside me as we follow our dreams and the unique calling that God has on our lives.

To Christy Bunnell (aka Crusty) ~ Guuuuurl! Thank you for pushing me to write a whole dang book! You have been the loudest and most persistent cheerleader throughout this entire process. You were always there with feedback and loads of encouragement and support. Thank you for believing in me and my message! XOXO

Made in the USA
Monee, IL
15 January 2020